For A... ...to the Piano

MW00817235

I Used to Play Piano

If you have studied piano before and want to play again, this book is for you. It includes music specifically selected for adults. You will review basic information as it appears in the music rather than through instructional exercises and text. After taking the first step to begin to play again, you will probably remember more than you think you do!

Enjoy!

Alfred

SINCE 1922

E. L. Lancaster / Victoria McArthur

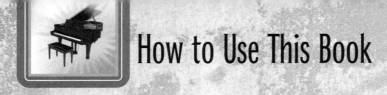

How to Use This Book

Getting Started

- Review the preliminary information on pages 6-9. If you are working with a teacher, you may want to review these concepts at your lesson.
- Check to see how much you remember by using the *What Do You Remember* section on pages 10–17. This section will help you determine the appropriate place to begin in the book.
- If you haven't played for a while, you can *get the fingers moving again* with the five-finger patterns, chords, cadences, scales and arpeggios on pages 18–19.

The Music

I Used to Play Piano is organized into units. Each unit contains music chosen from the following styles:

- Classical Arrangements—simplified arrangements of familiar classical themes
- Classical Masterworks—popular classical pieces written for the piano in their original versions
- Familiar Favorites—traditional pieces that are easily recognizable
- Popular Styles—pieces written in popular styles such as rock or ballad
- Jazz, Boogie, Blues, Ragtime—pieces written in one of these styles
- Studies—exercises or pieces to aid with developing technical facility

Some of the selections in this book were first composed for other collections. Because these pieces were so popular with adults, they are included in *I Used to Play Piano*. The original collections are cited at the bottom of each page of music. If you enjoy playing the pieces in this book, you may want to explore other pieces in the original collections.

If you want to play popular music from recordings, Broadway or the movies, the authors recommend:

> *Alfred's Basic Adult Piano Course Greatest Hits, Level 1* (#16505).

If you want to know more about music theory, the authors recommend:

> *Alfred's Essentials of Music Theory, Complete Book* (#17234) and its correlating CD-ROM Student Complete (#18833).

How to Work Through a Unit

- Within a given unit, select several pieces to study simultaneously. Choose pieces within the unit that you really like; feel free to skip others. The pieces in the units develop many skills needed for playing piano.
- After you have learned pieces in one unit, proceed to the next unit in a similar manner.
- Information about the composers and arrangers can be found on pages 148–149.

How to Work Through a Piece

- When beginning a new piece, review *Just the Facts* at the top of the page. If there are terms or concepts that are unfamiliar, consult the glossary (pages 150–151). Scan the piece and find where these terms appear in the music. In Units 1–3, some of these terms are identified in the music.
- In most pieces, you may first want to play hands separately to secure the notes and rhythms. When you feel comfortable, slowly begin to play hands together.
- Some pieces take longer to learn than others. Music is often written in sections much like verses and choruses in songs. Rather than trying to learn the entire piece at once, focus on one specific section for a few days. Such sections are labeled for effective practice—Practice Section 1 (PS1), etc.; look for sections that are similar or that repeat. Once you feel comfortable with one section, progress to the next one.
- Continue to work on the piece until you can play it confidently at an appropriate tempo without starting and stopping. Remember that slow practice is efficient to aid technical facility and music reading.

Evaluating Your Progress

- Progress will be faster if you are able to set aside time each day for regular practice.
- Shorter practice sessions (a minimum of 10–15 minutes) on a daily basis are more effective than longer periods of infrequent practice.
- Set long-range goals for learning specific pieces and then short-range goals on how to practice daily to achieve your objectives.
- Finally, have fun as you progress and share your music with family and friends.

Table of Contents

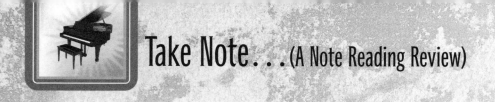

Take Note...(A Note Reading Review)

Note Names

Notes on the staff indicate **pitch**—the *highness* or *lowness* of the music tones.

Notes are named after the first seven letters of the alphabet: **A B C D E F G**

Key Names

Starting with the lowest white key, the piano keyboard has 88 keys, named A–G, in order.

The key names repeat over and over. (Some electronic instruments have fewer keys.)

Notes on the Staff

Music is written *on* the 5 lines and *in* the 4 spaces of the staff.

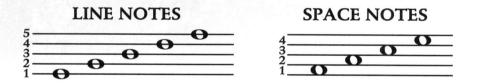

Notes are written on the staff in **treble clef** or **bass clef.**
Treble and bass staffs are connected by a **brace** to make the **grand staff.**
Leger lines are used above and below the staff to expand its range.

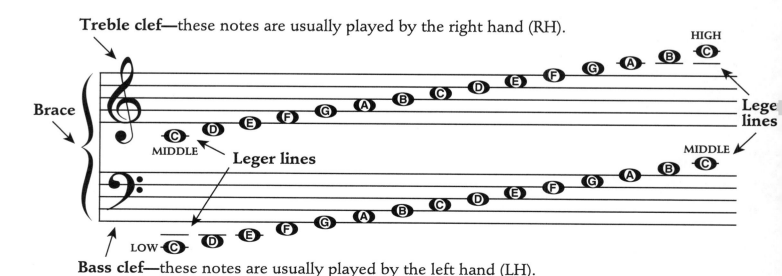

Reading Landmark Notes on the Grand Staff

Recognize these notes as **landmark notes** to aid with reading.

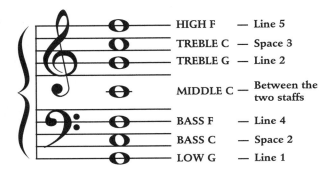

HIGH F — Line 5
TREBLE C — Space 3
TREBLE G — Line 2
MIDDLE C — Between the two staffs
BASS F — Line 4
BASS C — Space 2
LOW G — Line 1

Memorize each landmark note and learn to find its corresponding key on the keyboard quickly. Then you can read music by moving up or down from each landmark.

Review the landmark notes in the following order:

1.

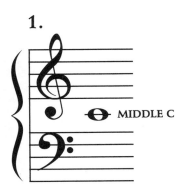

MIDDLE C

2.

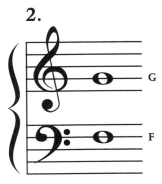

G

F

3.

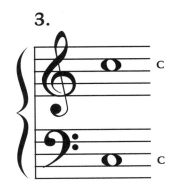

C

C

4.

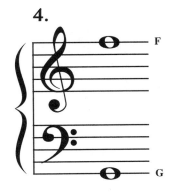

F

G

Reading Notes on the Staff

Notes move up (higher): 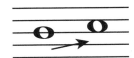   move down (lower):   repeat (same):

When notes *step* to the next line or space, use the next alphabet letter.

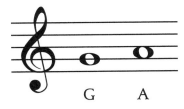

G   A

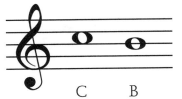

C   B

When notes *skip* a line or a space, skip an alphabet letter.

G to B

C to A

It's About Time...(A Rhythm Reading Review)

Pulse

Every piece of music has a steady **pulse** that is present throughout.
Sometimes pulse is called "the steady beat."

Rhythm

Notes indicate both pitch and **rhythmic duration.**
Rhythmic duration is measured in beats.
When learning and performing music, count the rhythm.

Duration

Notes		Rests		Beats (when ♩ = 1 beat)	
Whole note	𝅝	Whole rest	▬	4	beats
Dotted half note	𝅗𝅥.	Dotted half rest	▬·	3	beats
Half note	𝅗𝅥	Half rest	▬	2	beats
Dotted quarter note	♩.	Dotted quarter rest	𝄽·	1 ½	beats
Quarter note	♩	Quarter rest	𝄽	1	beat
Eighth note	♪	Eighth rest	𝄾	½	beat
Sixteenth note	♬	Sixteenth rest	𝄿	¼	beat

The Note Pyramid
Notice how the rows are equal.

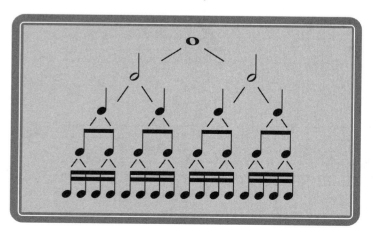

The Rest Pyramid
Notice how the rows are equal.

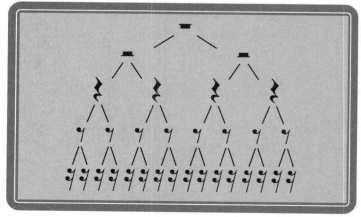

Tempo

Tempo is the speed of the pulse.
The tempo marking, written above the first measure of music (see below), tells the speed of the piece.

Time Signature (Meter)

Music has a **time signature** that tells how many beats are in each measure, and what kind of note gets one beat.

4/4 = 4 beats to each measure
4/4 = ♩ gets 1 beat

2/2 = 2 beats to each measure
2/2 = ♩ gets 1 beat

6/8 = 6 beats to each measure
6/8 = ♪ gets 1 beat

C (Common time) = **4/4**   **¢** (Cut time) = **2/2**

3/4 = 3 beats to each measure
3/4 = ♩ gets 1 beat

2/4 = 2 beats to each measure
2/4 = ♩ gets 1 beat

3/8 = 3 beats to each measure
3/8 = ♪ gets 1 beat

Measures are separated by **bar lines.**
A **double bar** is written at the end.
Notes and rests are arranged in various combinations to create rhythm patterns.

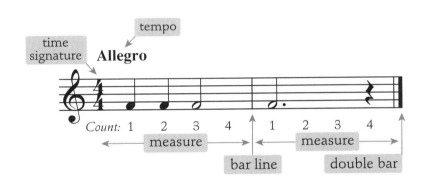

Putting a Finger on It...

- Don't let joints collapse as you play.
- Play on fingertip pads of fingers 2, 3, 4 and 5.
- Play on the sidetip of finger 1.
- Keep nails clipped to play with a good tone and fine technique.

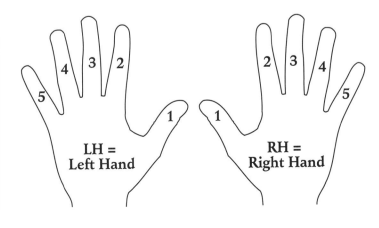

What Do You Remember? Part One

Use pages 10–17 to see what you remember and to determine where you should begin in this book.

1. Write the names of the notes on the lines. Then, play them on the keyboard.

a.
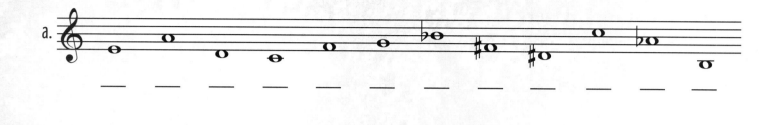

b.

c.
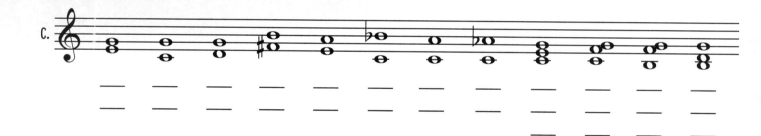

d.
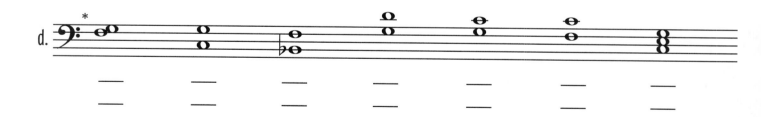

* If you need to review bass clef, the authors recommend: *Alfred's Basic Bass Clef* (6004).

2. Write the counts below each rhythm pattern. Then, tap and count aloud.

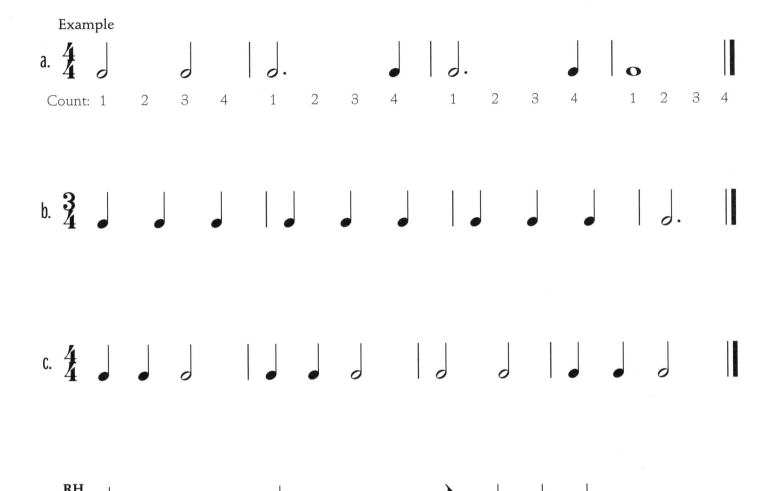

Example

a. $\frac{4}{4}$

Count: 1   2   3   4   1   2   3   4   1   2   3   4   1   2   3   4

b. $\frac{3}{4}$

c. $\frac{4}{4}$

d. RH $\frac{4}{4}$ LH

3. Sight read the music in Unit 1, pages 20–27.

See page 144 to check your answers.

If you need review on these things, begin your study with Unit 1, page 20.

If this was easy for you, proceed to *What Do You Remember? Part Two,* page 12.

What Do You Remember? Part Two

1. Write the names of the notes on the lines. Then, play the patterns on the keyboard.

a.

___ ___ ___   ___ ___ ___   ___

b.

___ ___ ___   ___ ___   ___

c.

___   ___
___   ___
___   ___

d.
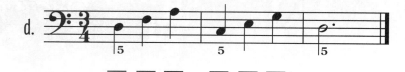
___ ___ ___   ___ ___ ___   ___

e.

___ ___ ___   ___ ___ ___   ___

f.

___ ___   ___

g.
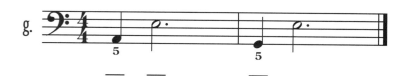
___ ___   ___

h.

___ ___ ___   ___ ___ ___   ___ ___ ___
___   ___   ___

2. Write the counts below each rhythm pattern. Then, tap and count aloud.

Example

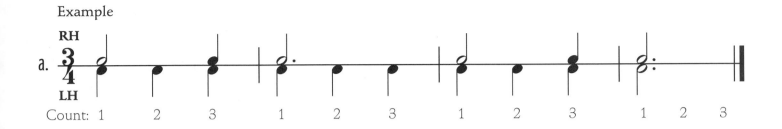

Count: 1   2   3   1   2   3   1   2   3   1   2   3

3. Sight read the music in Unit 2, pages 28–35.

See page 145 to check your answers.

If you need review on these things, begin your study with Unit 2, page 28.

If this was easy for you, proceed to *What Do You Remember? Part Three,* page 14.

What Do You Remember? Part Three

1. Write the names of the notes on the lines. Then, play the patterns on the keyboard.

a.

b.

c.

d.

e.

f.

g.

2. Write the counts below each rhythm pattern. Then, tap and count aloud.

3. Sight read the music in Unit 3, pages 36–45.

See page 146 to check your answers.

If you need review on these things, begin your study with Unit 3, page 36.

If this was easy for you, proceed to *What Do You Remember? Part Four,* page 16.

What Do You Remember? Part Four

1. Write the names of the notes on the lines. Then, play the patterns on the keyboard.

a.

b.

c.

d.

e.

f.

g.

(Play entire example with left hand.)

h.

i.

2. Write the counts below each rhythm pattern. Then, tap and count aloud.

Example

a. Count: 1 & 2 & 3 & 4 &   1 & 2 & 3 & 4 &   1 & 2 & 3 & 4 &   1 & 2 & 3 & 4 &

3. Sight read the music in Unit 4, pages 46–57.

See page 147 to check your answers.

If you need review on these things, begin your study with Unit 4, page 46.

If this was easy for you, begin your study with Unit 5, page 58.

Getting the Fingers Moving Again

You may have played some of the following patterns. Play any familiar ones to get your fingers moving again. You can also play them in other keys (transpose).

If you want to learn more scales, chords, arpeggios and cadences, the authors recommend Alfred's Basic Piano Library, *The First Book of Scales, Chords, Arpeggios & Cadences* (11761).

C Major Five-Finger Pattern and Chords

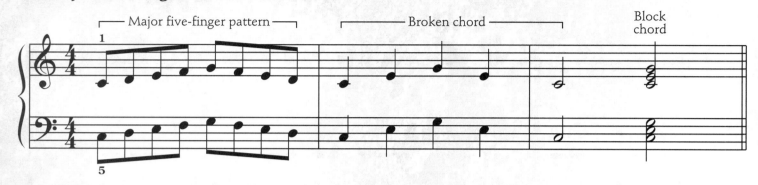

C Major Cadence

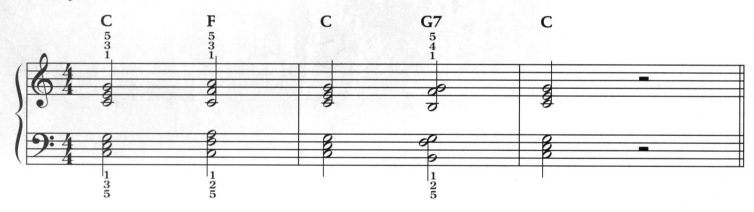

C Major Scale (2 octaves)*

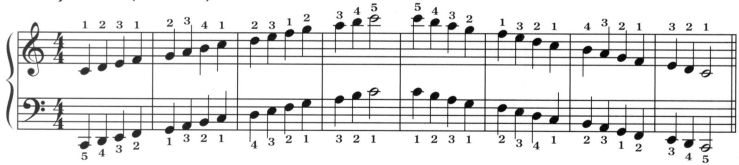

C Major Arpeggio (2 octaves)*

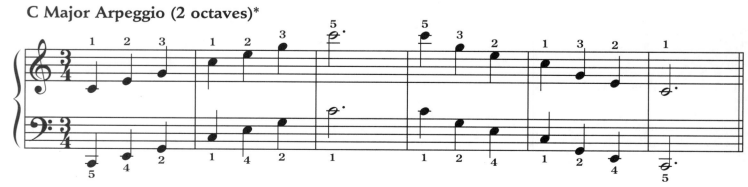

*You may first want to play the scales and arpeggios for only one octave.

A Minor Five-Finger Pattern and Chords

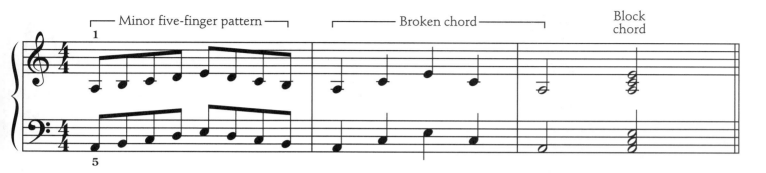

A Minor Cadence

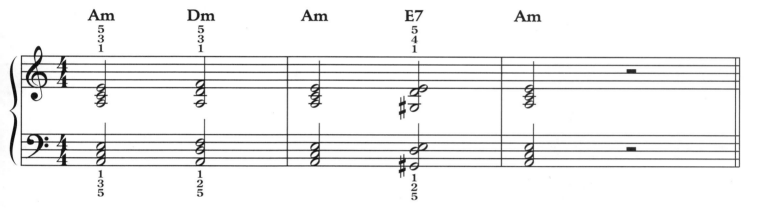

A Harmonic Minor Scale (2 octaves)*

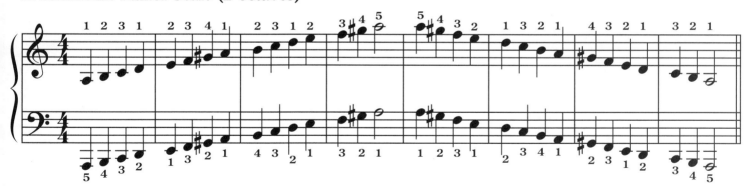

A Minor Arpeggio (2 octaves)*

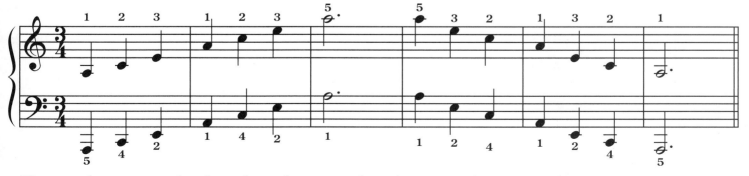

*You may first want to play the scales and arpeggios for only one octave.

Unit One

TRUMPET TUNE

Just the Facts

Key:	C major (no ♯s or ♭s)
Tempo:	Allegro
Dynamics:	*f*, ⟨, ⟩, *mp*
Other:	rit.

Jeremiah Clarke
Arr. by Margaret Goldston

Allegro
Practice Section 1 (PS1)

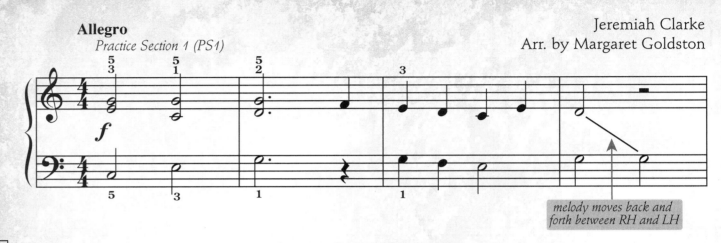

melody moves back and forth between RH and LH

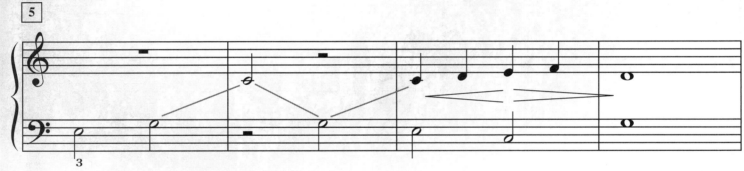

Practice Section 2 (PS2)

"Trumpet Tune" from *Simply Classic, Book 1,* by Margaret Goldston
Copyright © MCMXCII by Alfred Publishing Co., Inc.

LITTLE ROMANCE
(from *Musical ABC*)

Heinrich Wohlfahrt

Just the Facts

Key:	D minor (1 ♭—B♭)*
Tempo:	Andante con moto
Dynamics:	*p*, ⟨, ⟩, *mf*
Other:	phrase, ‖: :‖ , poco rit.

Andante con moto

Phrase—a musical thought; slur indicates legato (smoothly connected).

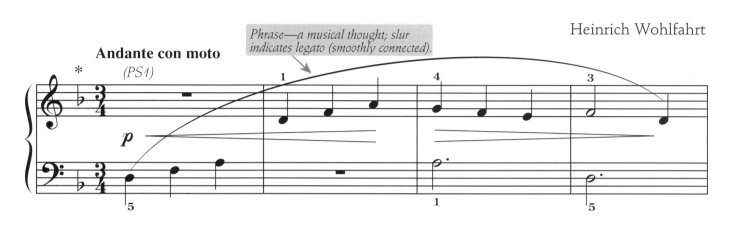

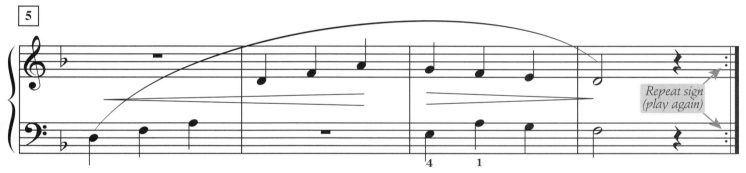

Repeat sign (play again)

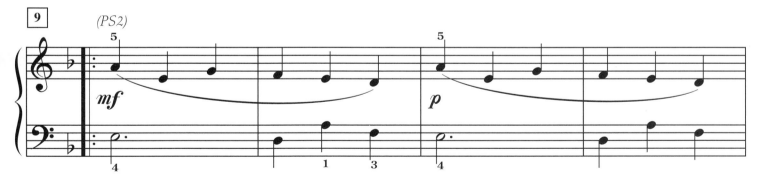

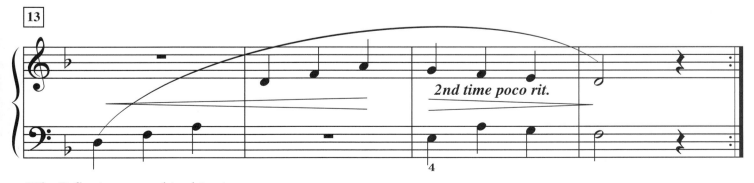

2nd time poco rit.

*The B-flat is not used in this piece.

BOOGIE TIME

Just the Facts

Key:	C major (no ♯s or ♭s)
Tempo:	Lively
Dynamics:	*mf*, *f*, <
Other:	slur, ♯, tie, $\dot{\bullet}$, ♮, ♭

Gayle Kowalchyk
E. L. Lancaster

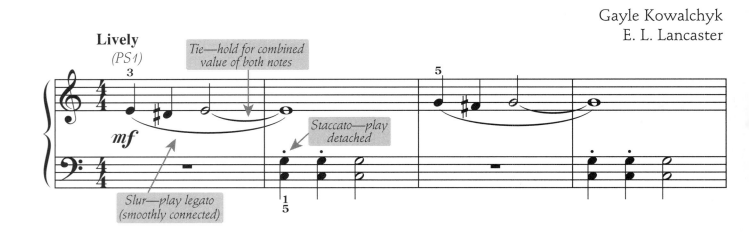

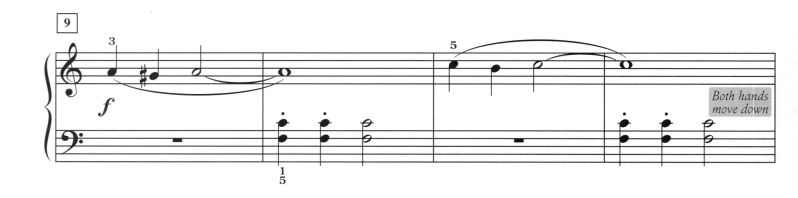

"Boogie Time" from *Boogie 'n' Blues, Book 1,* by Gayle Kowalchyk and E. L. Lancaster
Copyright © MCMXCI by Alfred Publishing Co., Inc.

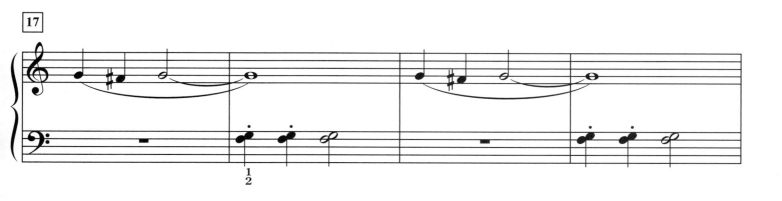

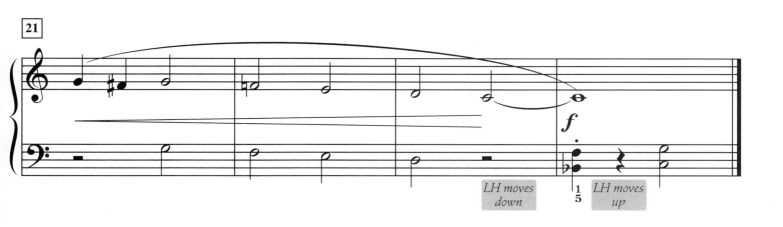

WHEN THE SAINTS GO MARCHING IN

Just the Facts

Key:	C major (no ♯s or ♭s)
Tempo:	Spirited march
Dynamics:	*mf*, *p*
Other:	♯, ♭, tie

Traditional
Arr. by Victoria McArthur

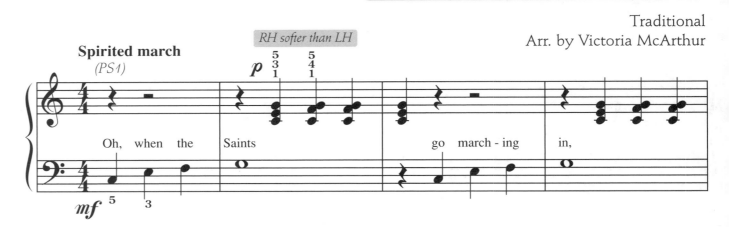

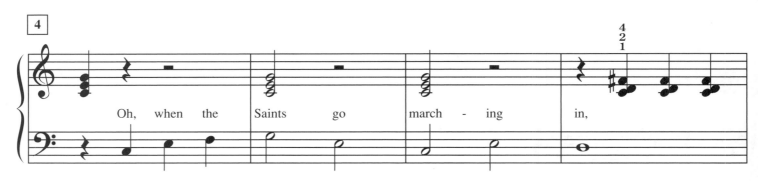

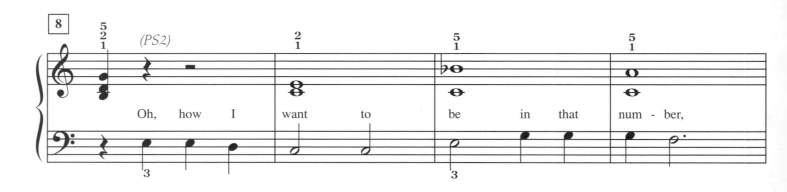

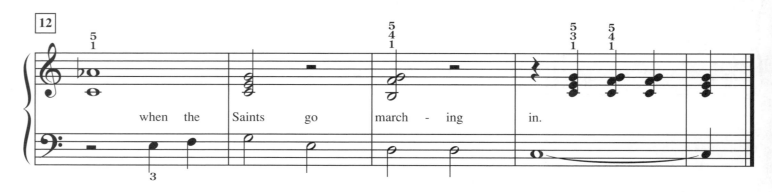

About the Damper Pedal

When the damper pedal is depressed, the felt dampers lift off the strings, allowing the sound to continue after the keys are released.

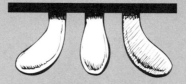

The damper pedal is on the right.

- Use the right foot on the damper pedal.
- Keep your heel on the floor.
- Let your ankle be relaxed as it gently pedals up and down.

For Exercises 1–2:

pedal down   pedal up

hold pedal down

For Exercise 3:

pedal down hold ∧ hold pedal up

pedal goes up, then down
to connect the sounds

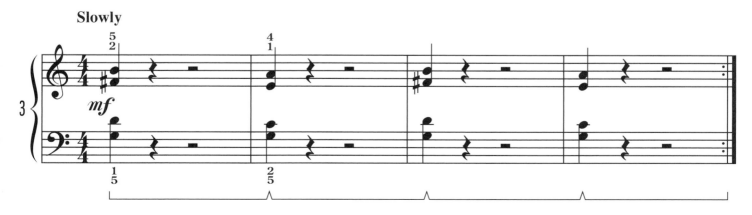

UNDER THE WILLOWS

Just the Facts

Key:	G major (1 ♯—F♯)
Tempo:	Allegro
Dynamics:	*mf*, ⟨, ⟩, *mp*, *p*, *pp*
Other:	⌐∧, slur, phrase, ♯, più, poco rit., tie

Randall Hartsell

"Under the Willows" from *Something Special, Book 1,* by Randall Hartsell
Copyright © MCMXC by Alfred Publishing Co., Inc.

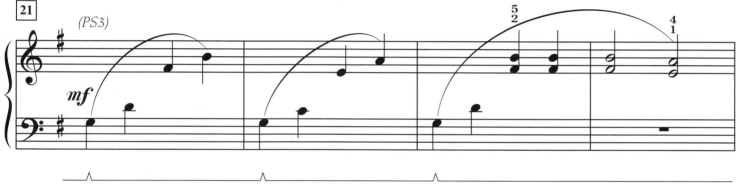

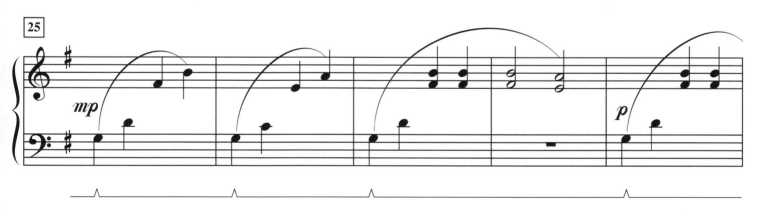

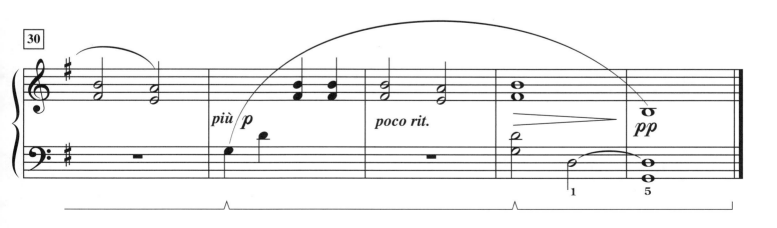

Unit Two

ANDANTINO

Just the Facts

Key:	C major (no #s or bs)
Tempo:	Andantino
Dynamics:	*mp*, *mf*, *f*, *p*, ⟨, ⟩
Other:	legato, slur, phrase

Louis Köhler

RONDEAU

(from *Suite de Symphonies, No. 1*)

Just the Facts

Key:	C major (no ♯s or ♭s)
Tempo:	Moderato
Dynamics:	*f*, *mp*, <
Other:	rondeau, ‖: :‖, tie, ⌐1.⌐ ⌐2.⌐, rit., 𝄐

Jean-Joseph Mouret
Arr. by Margaret Goldston

Fermata—hold note longer than full value

SCARBOROUGH FAIR

English Folk Song
Arr. by Victoria McArthur

Moderately, with feeling

8va—play one octave lower when under notes

ETUDES

I. For hands-together coordination with melody in RH

Cornelius Gurlitt
Op. 82, No. 10

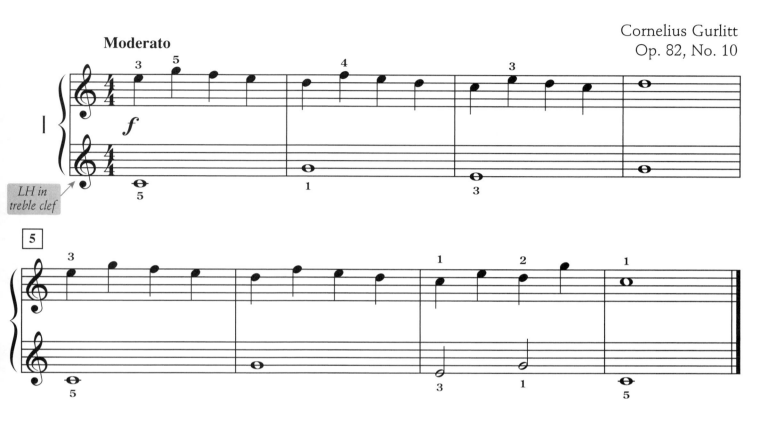

II. For hands-together coordination with melody in LH

Cornelius Gurlitt
Op. 82, No. 11

for Charles

BALLAD FOR A STARRY NIGHT

Just the Facts

Key:	C major (no ♯s or ♭s)
Tempo:	With tender feeling
Dynamics:	*p*, cresc., *f*, *mp*
Other:	⌐⌐⌐ , tie, slur, simile, poco rit., 8va, 𝄐

Victoria McArthur

With tender feeling
(PS1)

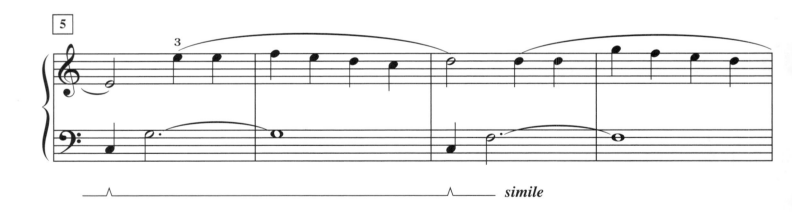

simile

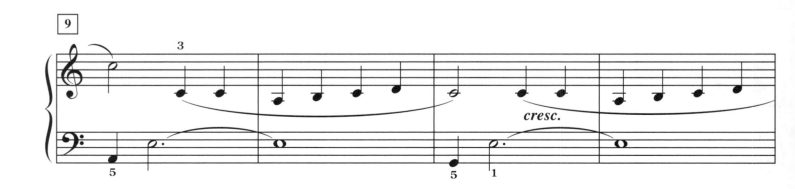

cresc.

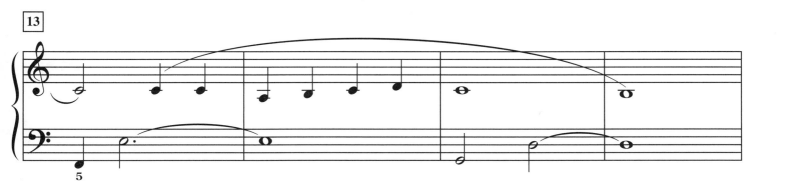

17 **A little slower**
(PS2)

21

25

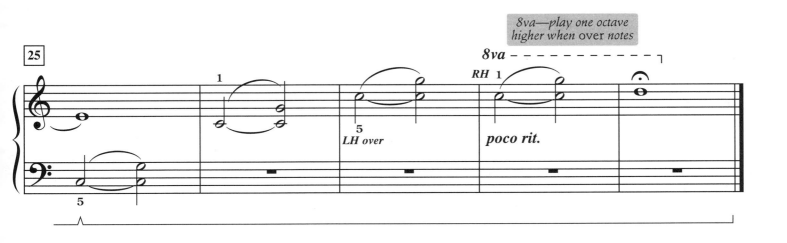

8va—play one octave higher when over notes

BLUES TRAIN

Just the Facts

Key:	C major (no ♯s or ♭s)
Tempo:	Chugging along, moderately fast and steadily
Dynamics:	*f*
Other:	♭, ♮, tie, ♯, $\overset{>}{\rho}$, rit. e dim. poco a poco

Catherine Rollin

Chugging along, moderately fast and steadily

Accent sign—play louder

rit. e dim. poco a poco

Unit Three

THEME FROM EINE KLEINE NACHTMUSIK
(A Little Night Music)

Just the Facts

Key:	C major (no ♯s or ♭s)
Tempo:	Allegro
Dynamics:	*f*, <, *mp*, >, *p*, *p-mp*
Other:	slur, tie, ‖: :‖, 1. 2., $\bar{\rho}$, $\overset{>}{\rho}$

Wolfgang Amadeus Mozart
Arr. by Margaret Goldston

Allegro

*Play all quarter notes detached except where otherwise indicated.

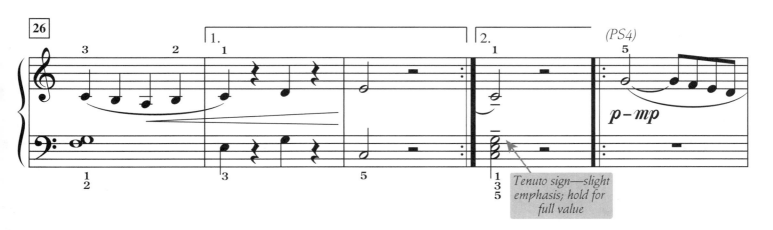

Tenuto sign—slight emphasis; hold for full value

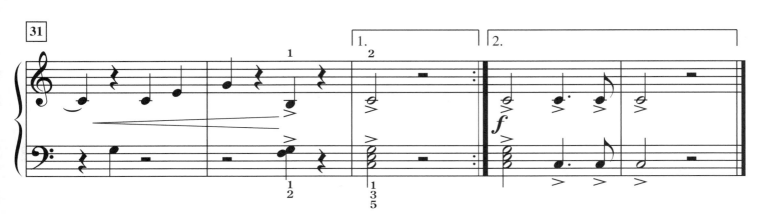

QUADRILLE

Just the Facts

Key:	C major (no ♯s or ♭s)
Tempo:	Allegretto
Dynamics:	*f*, *mf*
Other:	quadrille, slur, LH detached, , |: :|

Franz Joseph Haydn

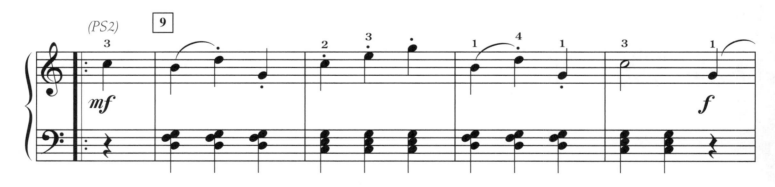

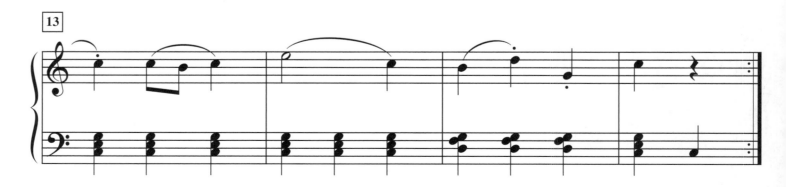

ETUDES

(from the *Preparatory School*)

I. For even voicing of 3rds in RH; slur gesture in LH

Ferdinand Beyer
Op. 101, No. 68

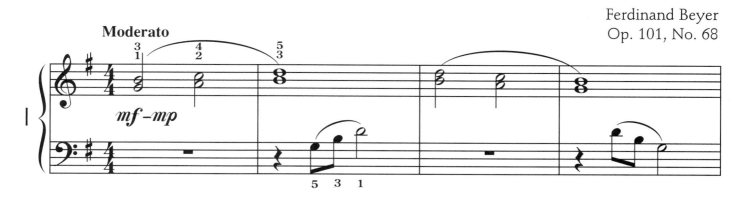

II. For even voicing of 3rds in LH; slur gesture in RH

Ferdinand Beyer
Op. 101, No. 69

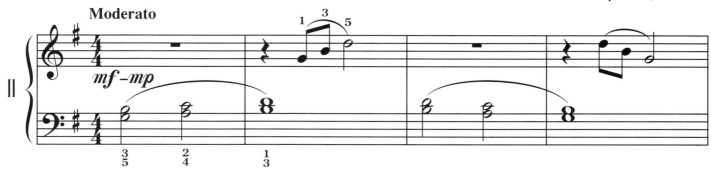

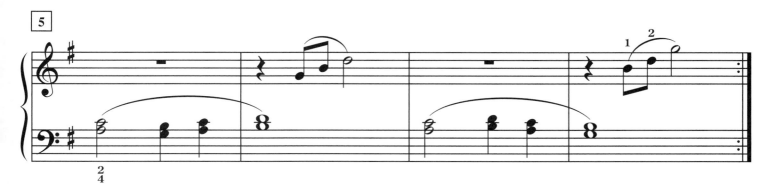

LA BAMBA

Just the Facts

Key:	C major (no ♯s or ♭s)
Tempo:	With energy
Dynamics:	*mf*, ⦤, *f*, *mp*, *ff*
Other:	slur, 𝆏, 𝆏

Mexican Folk Tune
Arr. by Carol Matz

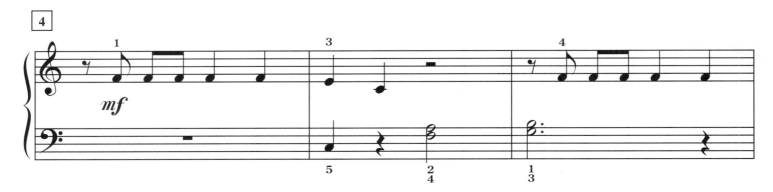

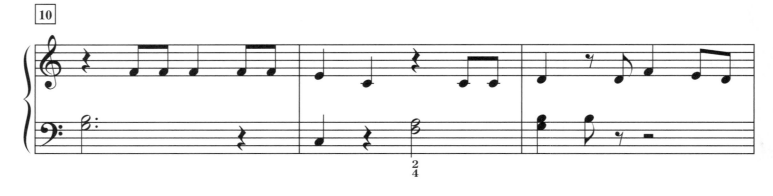

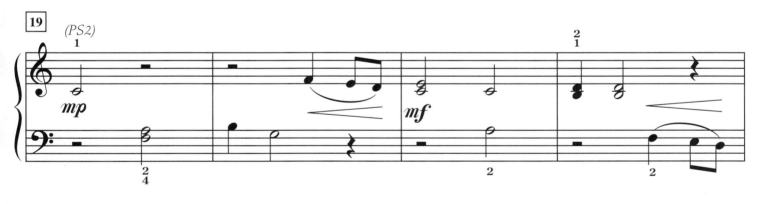

DREAM ECHOES

Just the Facts

Key:	G major (1 ♯—F♯)
Tempo:	Reflective
Dynamics:	*mf*, *mp*, ⟨, ⟩
Other:	⌐⌐ , phrase, rit., 𝄐, a tempo, 8va

E. L. Lancaster

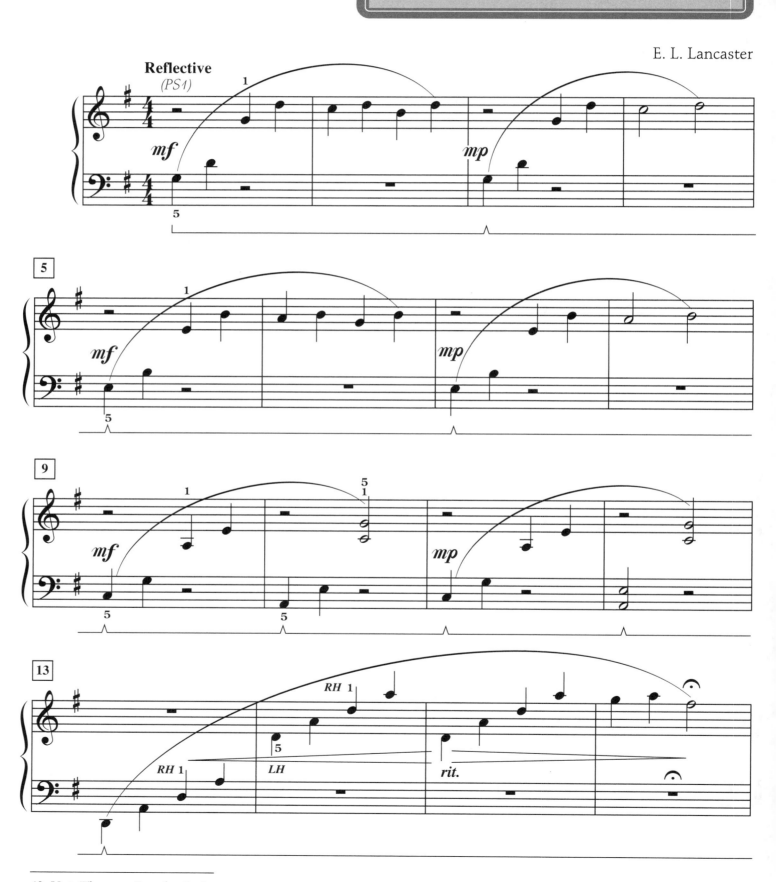

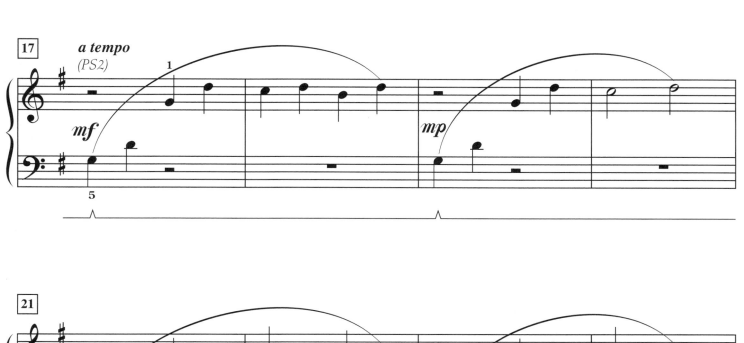

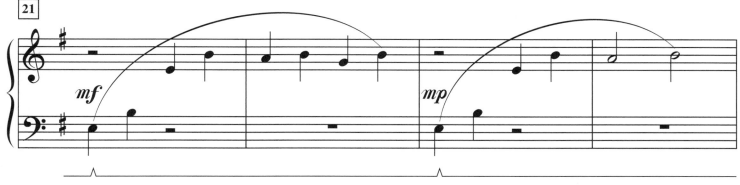

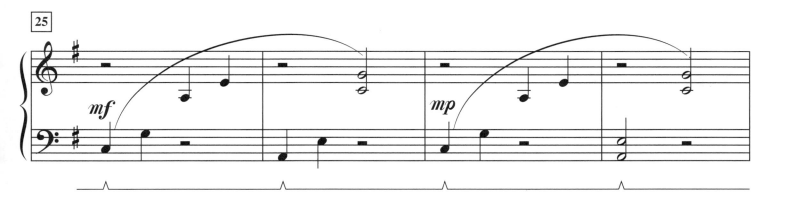

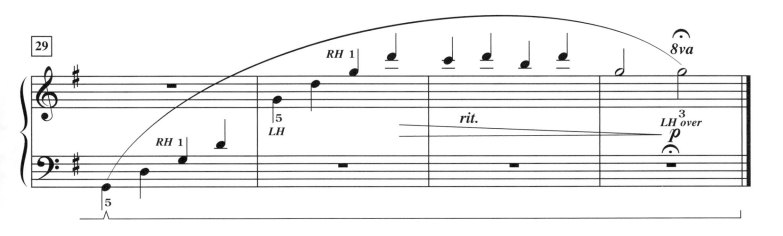

CELEBRATION BOOGIE

Just the Facts

Key:	G major (1 ♯—F♯)
Tempo:	Solidly
Dynamics:	*mf*, *f*, ＜
Other:	LH detached, ♯, ♮, phrase, tie, slur, ♭, 8va

Gayle Kowalchyk
E. L. Lancaster

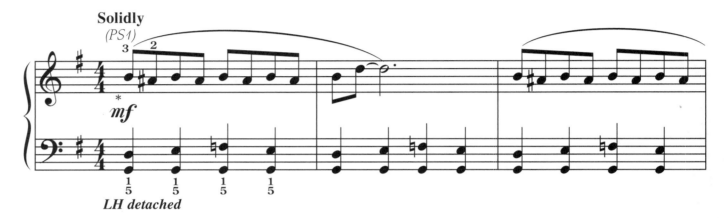

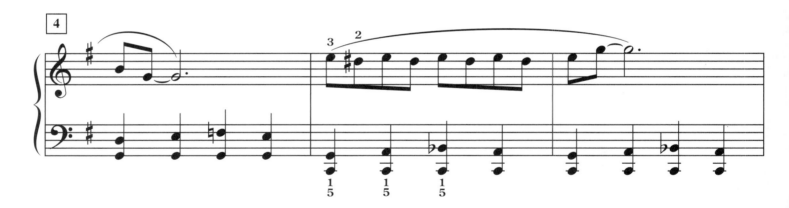

*You may play the eighth notes
a bit unevenly (with swing):   long short long short *etc.*

"Celebration Boogie" from *Boogie 'n' Blues, Book 2,* by Gayle Kowalchyk and E. L. Lancaster
Copyright © MCMXCIII by Alfred Publishing Co., Inc.

Unit Four

POLOVETSIAN DANCE
(from *Prince Igor*)

Just the Facts

Key:	G major (1 ♯ — F♯)
Tempo:	Moderately
Dynamics:	*mp*, <, *mf*, >, *p*
Other:	⌐⌐⌐ , phrase, tie, slur, ♭, ♯, rit.

Alexander Borodin
Arr. by Carol Matz

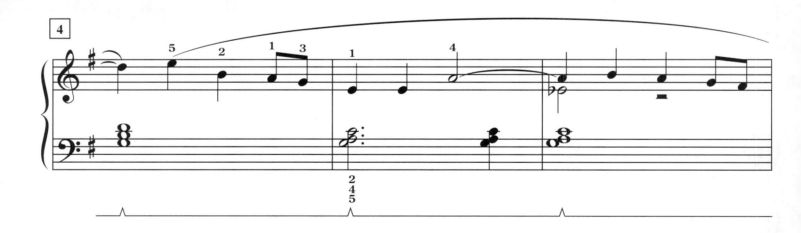

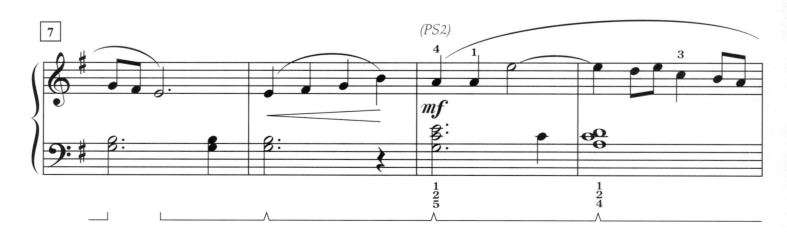

DISTANT BELLS

Jean-Louis Streabbog
Op. 63, No. 6

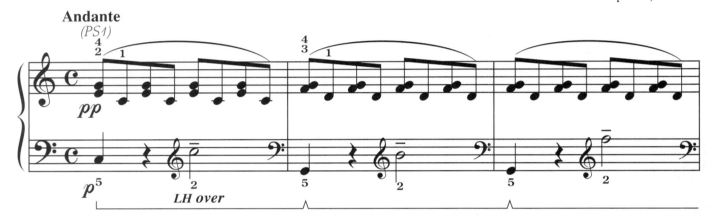

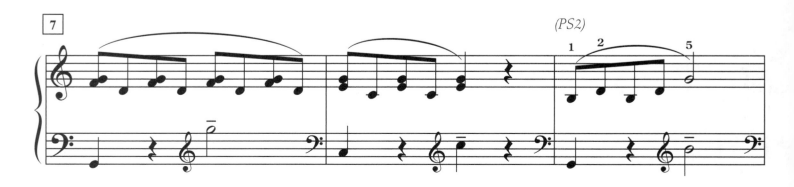

EXERCISE NO. 1
(from *The Virtuoso Pianist*)
For finger independence and dexterity

Charles-Louis Hanon
Simplified

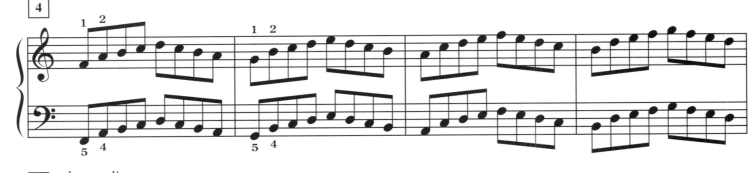

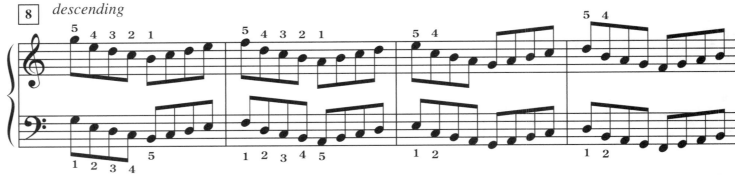

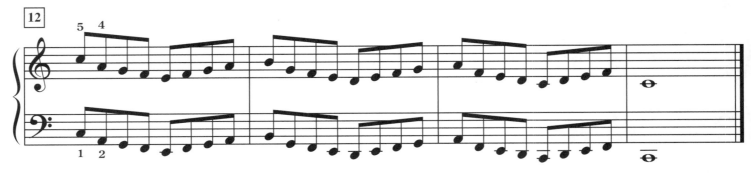

EXERCISE NO. 2
(from *The Virtuoso Pianist*)
For finger independence and dexterity

Charles-Louis Hanon
Simplified

ascending

descending

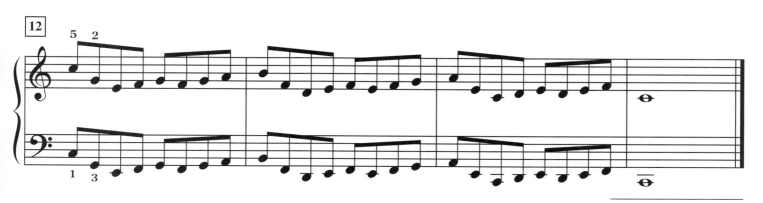

TAKE ME OUT TO THE BALL GAME

Words by Jack Norworth
Music by Albert Von Tilzer
Arr. by Victoria McArthur

Just the Facts

Key:	F major (1 ♭—B♭)
Tempo:	Moderately
Dynamics:	*mf*, <, >, *f*
Other:	phrase, tie, ♯, ♮, ♭, >, ⌣

Moderately
(PS1)

Take me out to the ball game,

take me out to the crowd.

Buy me some pea - nuts and Crack - er Jacks;

I don't care if I nev - er get back. Let me

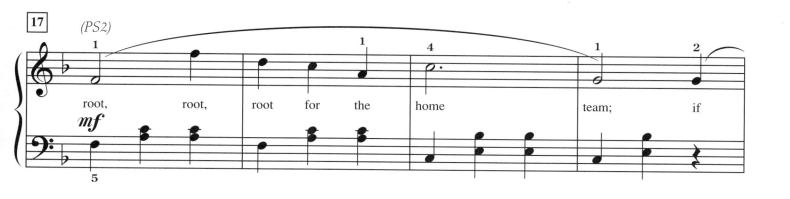

root,   root,   root   for   the   home   team;   if

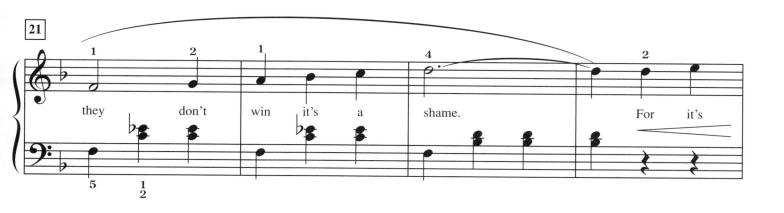

they   don't   win   it's   a   shame.   For   it's

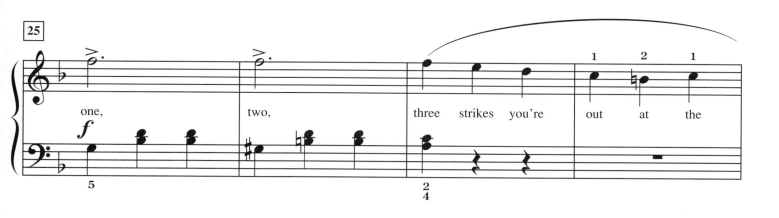

one,   two,   three   strikes   you're   out   at   the

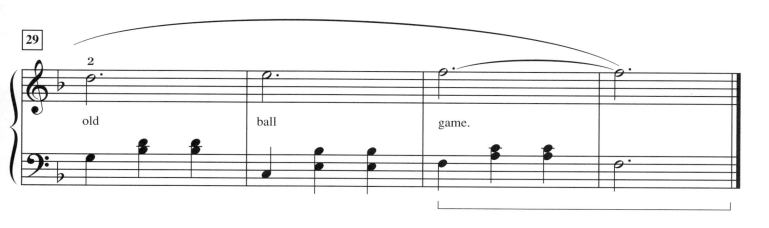

old   ball   game.

MOONLIT SHORES

Just the Facts

Key:	C major (no ♯s or ♭s)
Tempo:	Moderato
Dynamics:	*mp*, <, >, *f*, *mf*, *p*, *pp*
Other:	⌐∧⌐, slur, simile, poco rit., a tempo, più, tie

Randall Hartsell

GOT THOSE BOOGIE BLUES

Just the Facts

Key:	C major (no ♯s or ♭s)
Tempo:	Allegro
Dynamics:	*f*, >, *mp*, *mf*, <
Other:	slur, ♩·, ♯, ♭, ♮, tie, 1. ⌐, phrase, to next strain, 2. ⌐, ⌐___⌐, rit., Fine, D. C. al Fine

Dennis Alexander

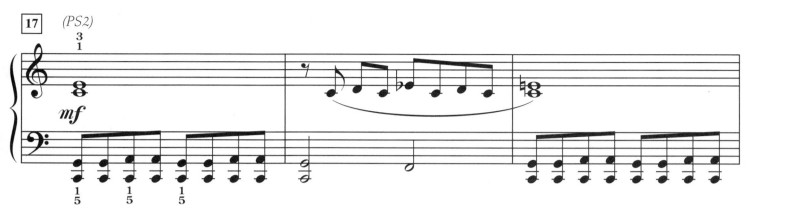

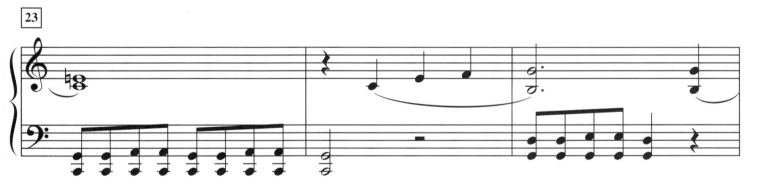

Unit Five

FÜR ELISE
(For Elise)

Just the Facts

Key:	A minor (no ♯s or ♭s)
Tempo:	With expression
Dynamics:	p, mp, cresc., dim.
Other:	WoO, phrase, ♯, ♮, slur, ⌐___, 8va, poco rit.

Ludwig van Beethoven
WoO 59
Arr. by Victoria McArthur

With expression

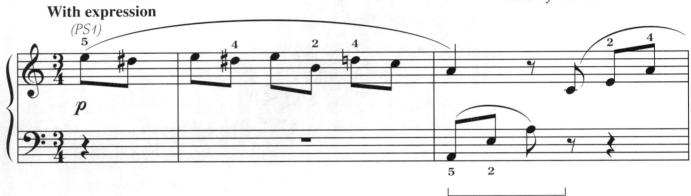

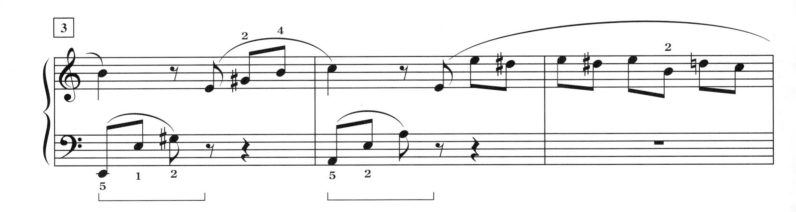

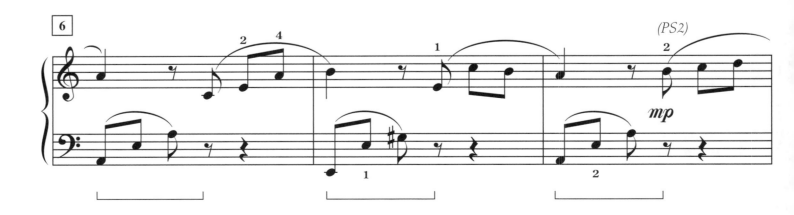

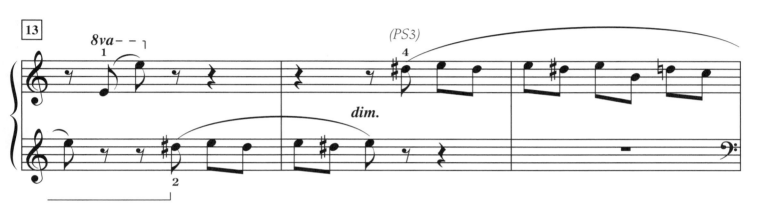

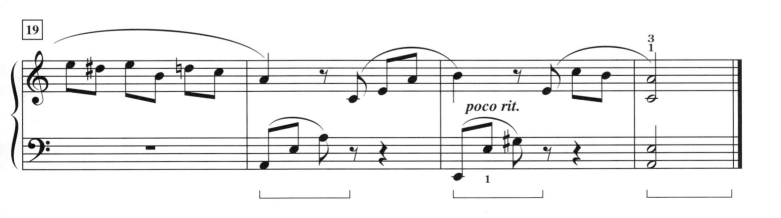

MINUET IN G MAJOR

(from the *Notebook for Anna Magdalena*)

Just the Facts

Key:	G major (1 ♯—F♯)
Tempo:	Allegro moderato
Dynamics:	*mf*, ⟍, *mp*, ⟋, *f*
Other:	minuet, slur, ♪̇, appoggiatura (♪♩.), ‖: :‖, ♯, ♮

Johann Sebastian Bach*

Allegro moderato

* Although this piece is often attributed to Johann Sebastian Bach, recent scholarship suggests that it was actually written by Christian Pezold (1677–c. 1733), a German organist and composer.

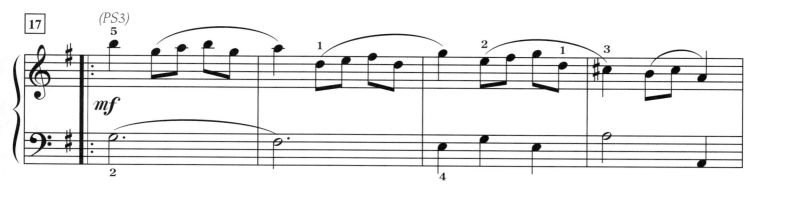

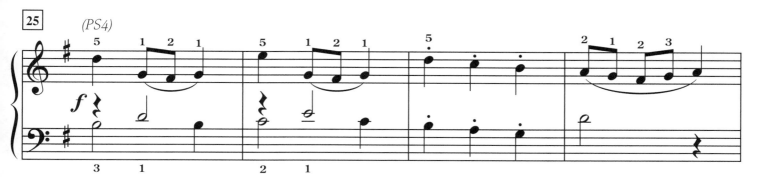

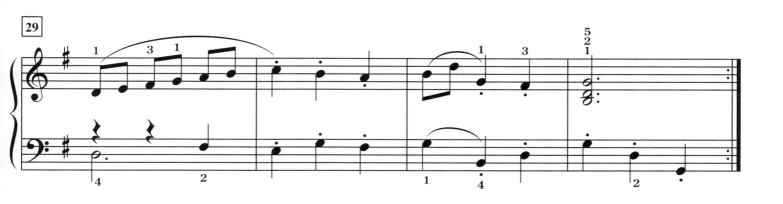

SIMPLE GIFTS

Just the Facts

Key:	F major (1 ♭—B♭)
Tempo:	Somewhat slowly
Dynamics:	*mf*
Other:	phrase, ⌐⌐⌐, ♯, ♭, ⌢, a tempo, poco rit.

Shaker Melody
Arr. by Victoria McArthur

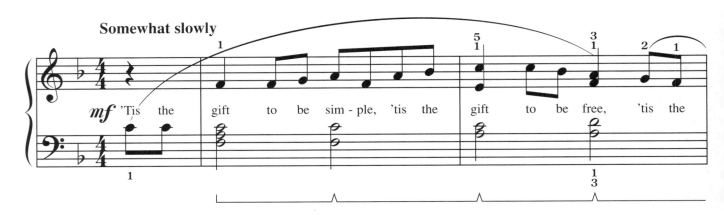

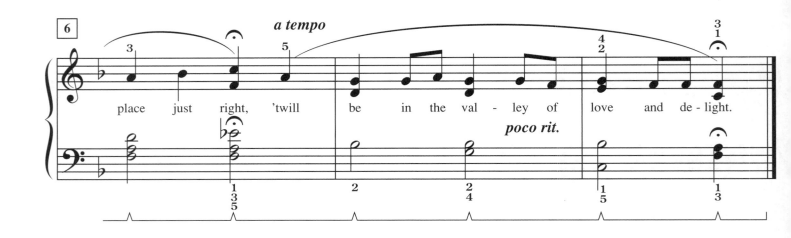

EXERCISE NO. 10

(from *A Piano Method*)

For finger independence and dexterity

Adolphe-Clair Le Carpentier

Practice Hints

Use the practice hints on page 50.

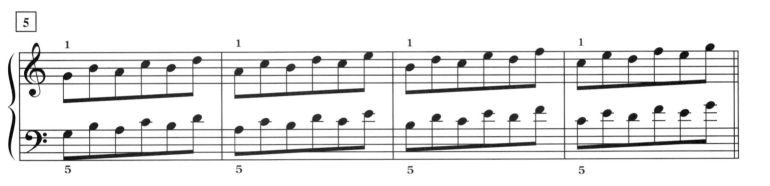

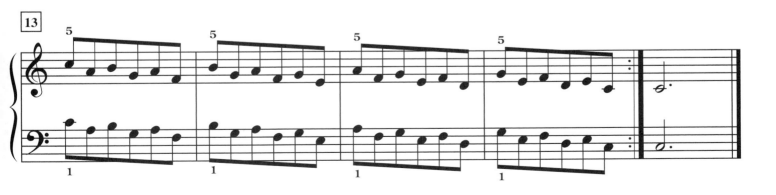

FAR FROM HOME

<table>
<tr><td>Just the Facts</td></tr>
</table>

Just the Facts

Key:	C major (no ♯ or ♭)
Tempo:	Gently
Dynamics:	*mf*, *p*, <, *f*, >, *mp*
Other:	slur, ⌐∧⌐ , rit., tie

Dennis Alexander

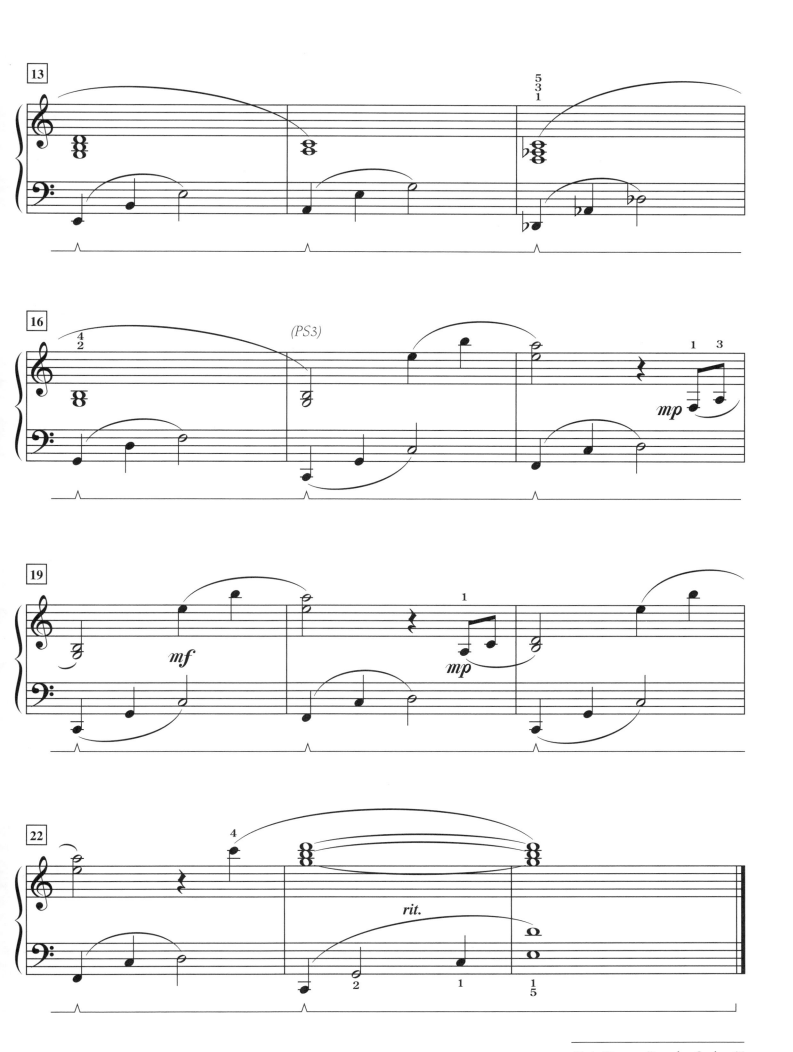

DON'T WANNA LEAVE YOU BLUES

Just the Facts

Key:	C major (no ♯s or ♭s)
Tempo:	Mournfully, with slow blues swing
Dynamics:	*mf*, <, >, *f*, *mp*, *p*
Other:	♫ = ♩³♪, phrase, tie, ♭, ♮, ♯, >, ♪♪♪, rit., ⌐⌐, 𝄐, 𝄼

Martha Mier

Mournfully, with slow blues swing (♫ = ♩³♪)

(PS3)

Unit Six

THEME FROM CONCERTO NO. 2
(Third Movement)

Sergei Rachmaninoff
Op. 18
Arr. by Victoria McArthur

Just the Facts

Key:	C major (no ♯s or ♭s)
Tempo:	Moderately slow
Dynamics:	*mp*, cresc., *mf*, dim.
Other:	concerto, Op., ⌴⌃⌴, phrase, tie, ♭, ♯

RONDINO

Just the Facts

Key:	C major (no ♯s or ♭s)
Tempo:	Moderato
Dynamics:	*mf*, *p*, *f*
Other:	rondino, legato, poco rit., tie, :‖, Fine, ♯, slur, D. C. al Fine

Moderato

RH legato

Jean-Philippe Rameau

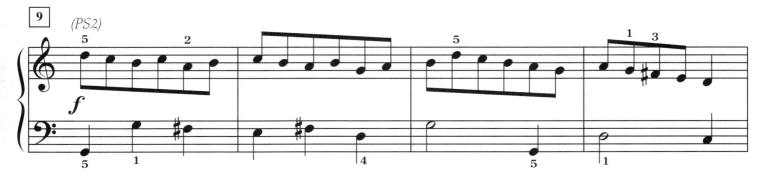

for Carol Taff

AMAZING GRACE

Virginia Harmony
Words by John Newton and John P. Rees
Arr. by Victoria McArthur

Slowly, with deep feeling

STUDY

For voicing LH melody over RH chords

Just the Facts

Key:	G major (1 ♯—F♯)
Tempo:	Moderato
Dynamics:	*mf*, *p*, >, *mp*, *pp*, <
Other:	Op., slur, phrase, tie, ♯, ♮, poco rit.

Ludvig Schytte
Op. 108, No. 12

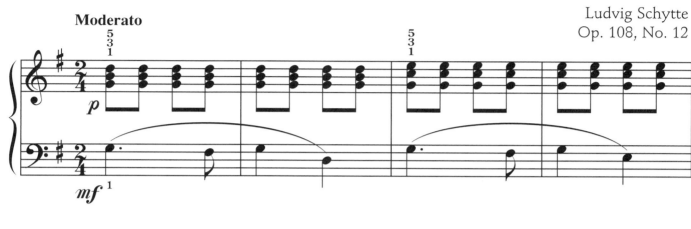

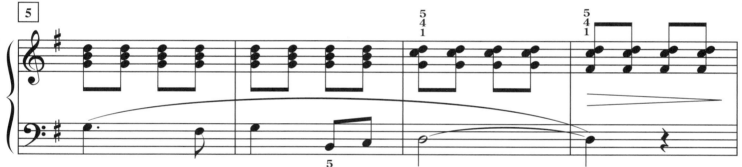

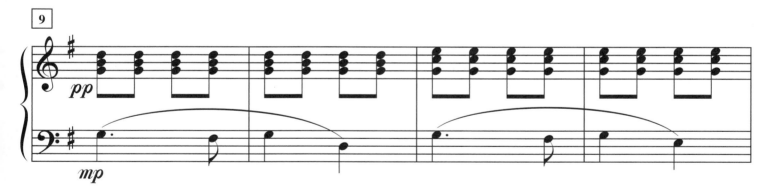

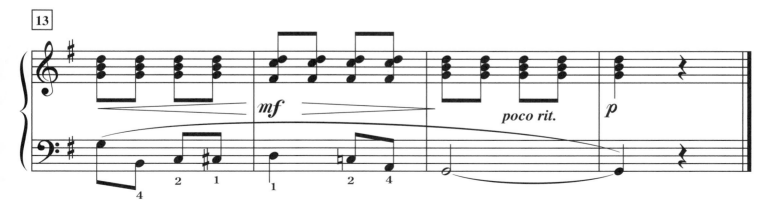

AUTUMN SUNSET

Just the Facts

Key:	G major (1 ♯—F♯)
Tempo:	Flowing
Dynamics:	*p*, cresc., *mf*, dim., *pp*, <, *mp*, >
Other:	└─∧─┘ , slur, ♭, simile, phrase, tie, ♯, rall., a tempo, riten., 𝄐

George Peter Tingley

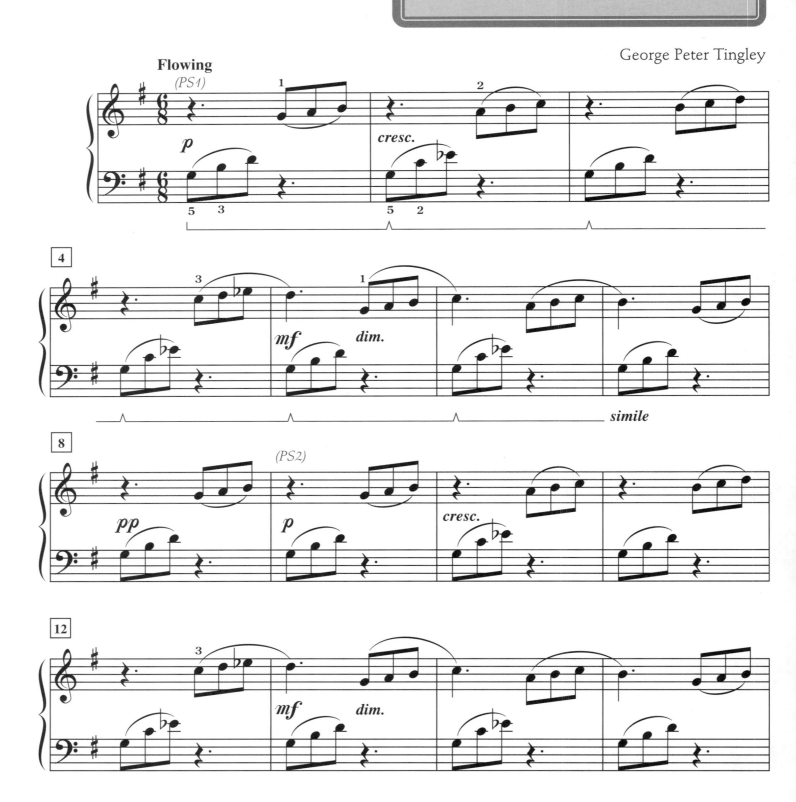

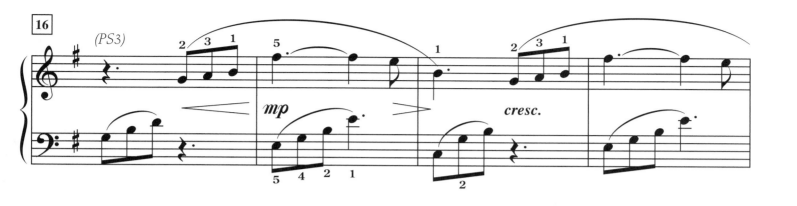

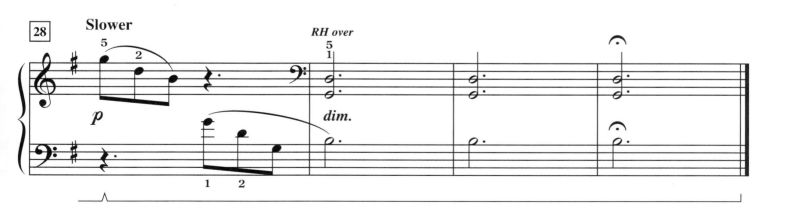

JUST STRUTTIN' ALONG

Just the Facts

Key: A minor (no ♯s or ♭s)
Tempo: Moderate blues swing
Dynamics: *mp*, *p*, ⟨, *mf*, *f*, ⟩, *pp*
Other: ♫ = ⌐♩³♪⌐, ♩, ♩, tie, slur, ♯, ♮, ⌐⌐, ⌢

Martha Mier

Unit Seven

JESU, JOY OF MAN'S DESIRING

(from *Cantata No. 147*)

Just the Facts

Key: G major (1 ♯—F♯)
Tempo: Moderately flowing and simple
Dynamics: *mp*, ⟨, *f*, ⟩, *mf*
Other: cantata, ♪♫, ⌐⌐, phrase, simile, ♯, rit.

Johann Sebastian Bach
Arr. by E. L. Lancaster

Moderately flowing and simple

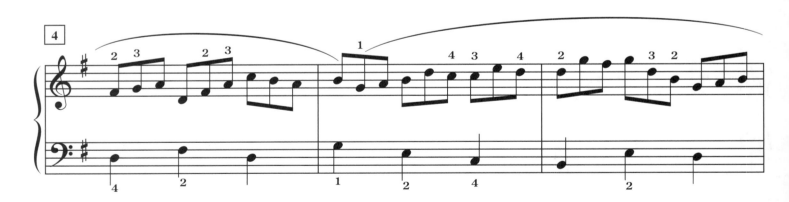

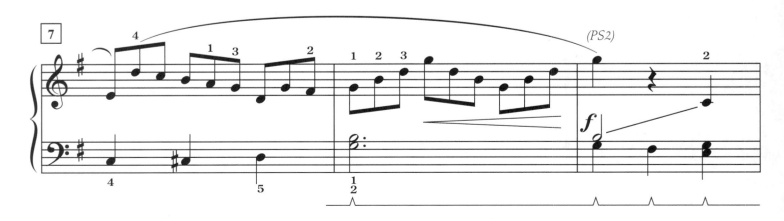

MUSETTE IN D MAJOR

(from the *Notebook for Anna Magdalena*)

Just the Facts

Key:	D major (2 ♯s—F♯, C♯)
Tempo:	Allegretto
Dynamics:	*mf*, *mp*, *p*, cresc., *f*
Other:	musette, LH detached, slur, ♩·, ‖: :‖

Johann Sebastian Bach*

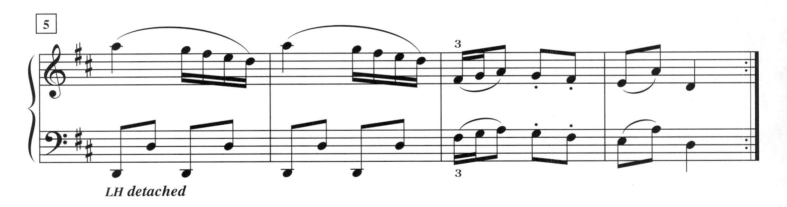

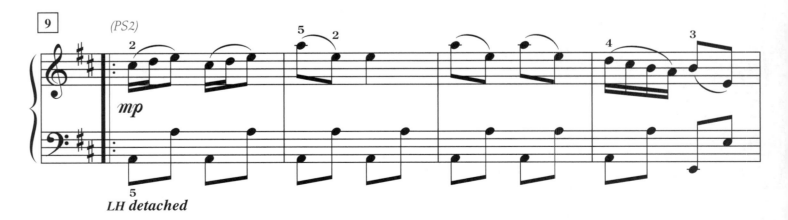

*Although this piece is often attributed to Johann Sebastian Bach and is included in the *Notebook for Anna Magdalena,* recent scholarship suggests that it may have been written by someone other than Bach.

THE RIDDLE SONG

(I Gave My Love a Cherry)

Just the Facts

Key: G major (1 ♯—F♯)
Tempo: Flowing
Dynamics: *mp*, <, >, *mf*
Other: ⌐⌐⌐⌐, phrase, ♮, poco rit., 𝄐

Appalachian Song
Arr. by Carol Matz

PRELUDE IN G MINOR

For five-finger patterns, broken chords
and chromatic scales

Just the Facts

Key:	G minor (2 ♭s—B♭, E♭)
Tempo:	Allegro
Dynamics:	*mf*, *p*, cresc., *f*
Other:	prelude, Op., slur, phrase, $\dot{\cdot}$, ♮, ♯, ⌐, ♭, $\bar{\dot{\cdot}}$, ⌢

Giuseppe Concone
Op. 37, No. 6

REMEMBER WHEN

Just the Facts

Key:	C major (no ♯s or ♭s)
Tempo:	Andante cantabile
Dynamics:	*mf*, >, *mp*, *f*
Other:	⌐⌐, slur, phrase, ♭, tie, 8va., rit.

Andante cantabile
(PS1)

Dennis Alexander

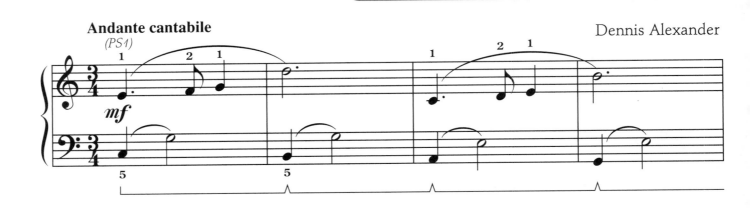

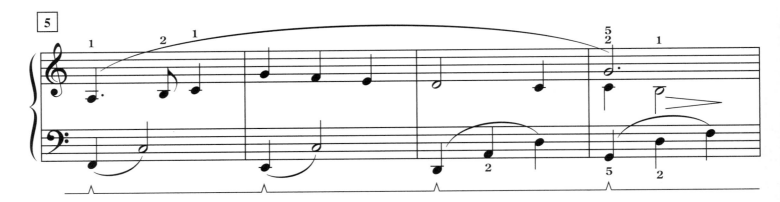

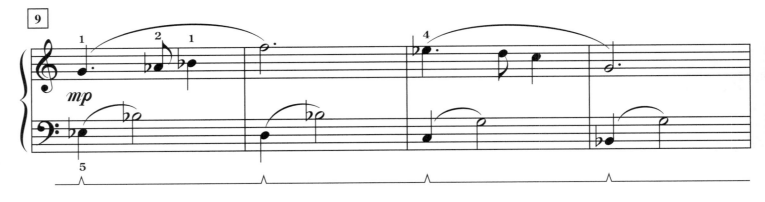

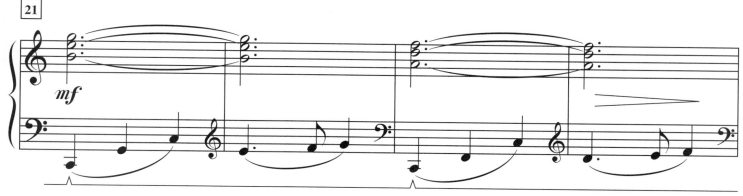

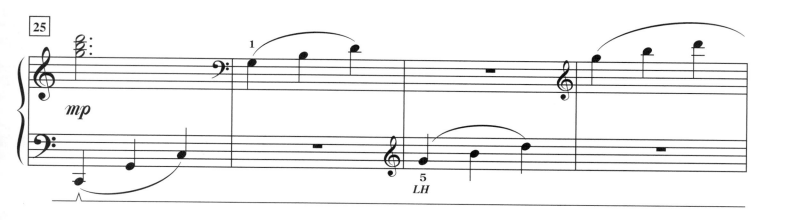

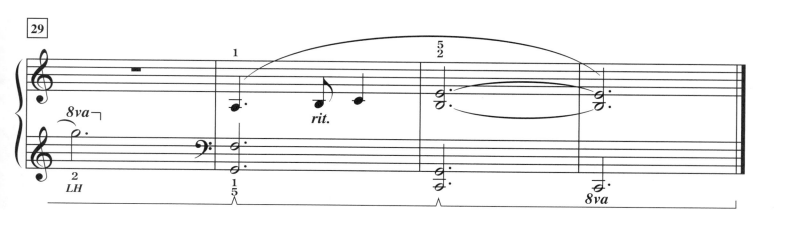

NEW WORLD DISCOVERY

Just the Facts

Key:	A minor (no #s or ♭s)
Tempo:	Fast, festive
Dynamics:	*mf*, *mp*, <, >, *f*, cresc., *ff*
Other:	▭, slur, rit., #, tie, ⏊, ⌢, •, phrase

Martha Mier

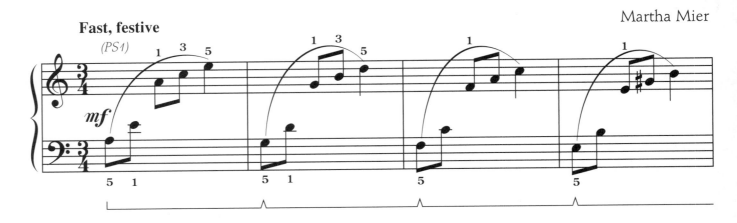

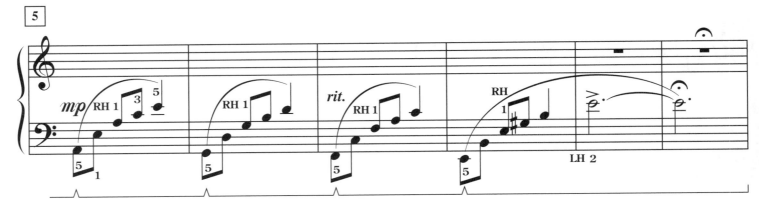

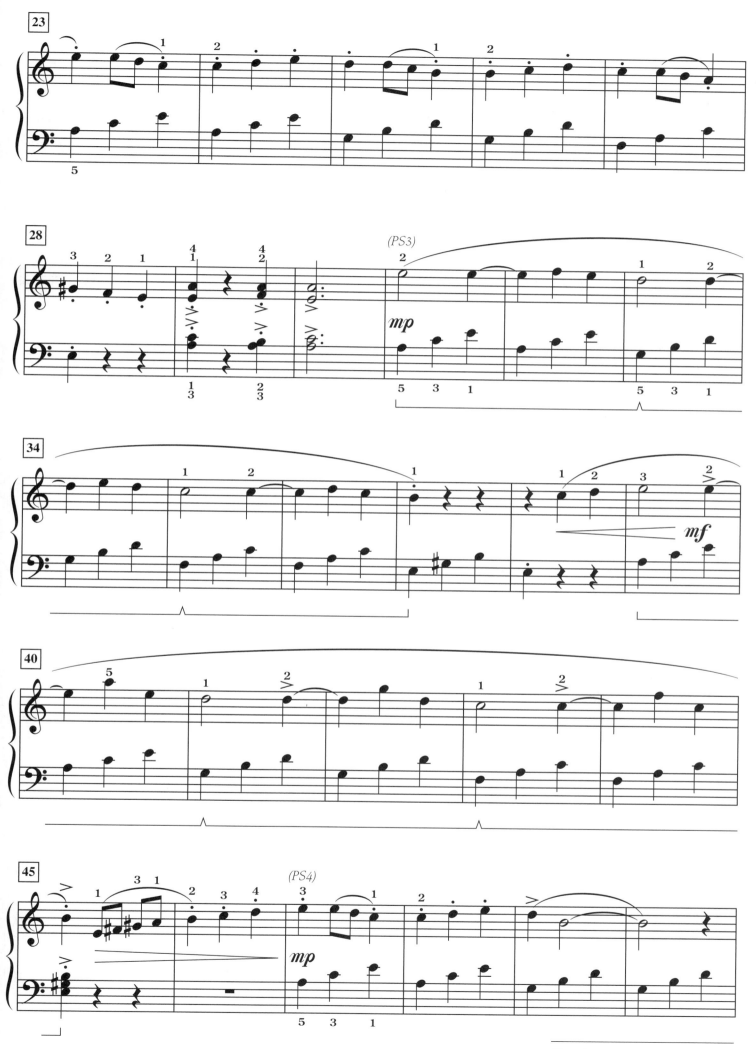

Unit Eight

CLAIR DE LUNE
(from *Suite Bergamasque*)

Just the Facts

Key:	C major (no ♯s or ♭s)
Tempo:	Andante
Dynamics:	*pp*, <, >, *p*, *mp*, *mf*, dim.
Other:	⌐⌐, slur, tie, ♯, ♮, ♭, rit., 8va, {

Claude Debussy
Arr. by E. L. Lancaster

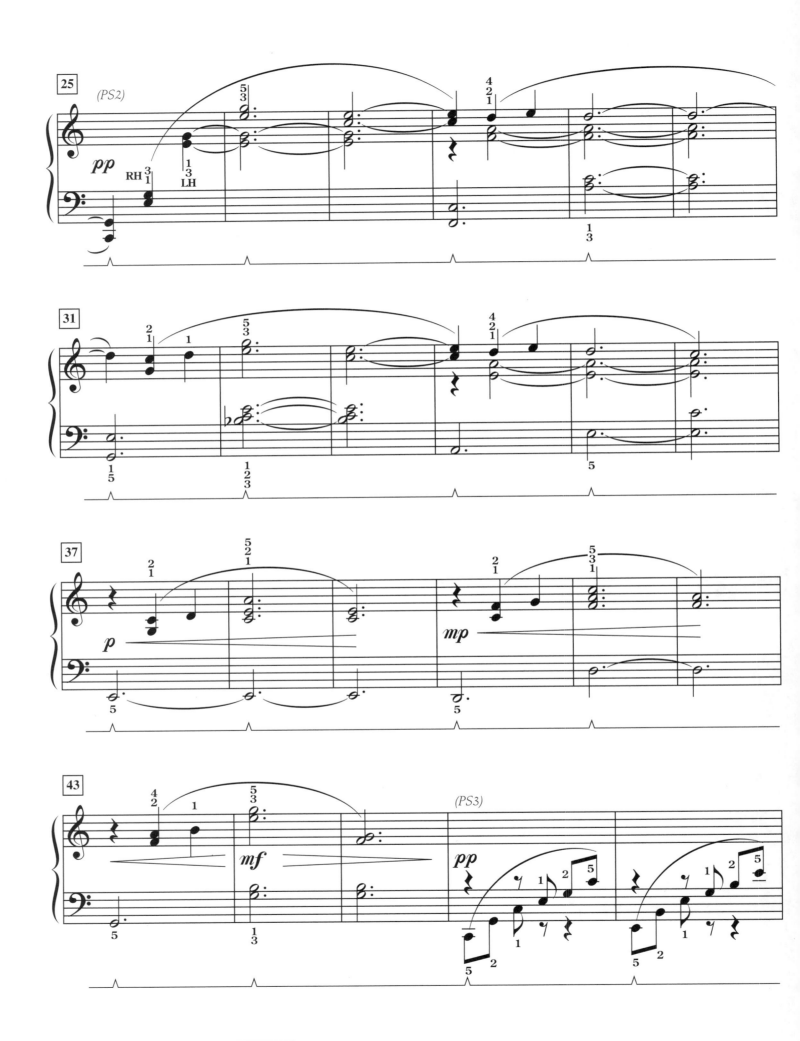

St. Louis Blues

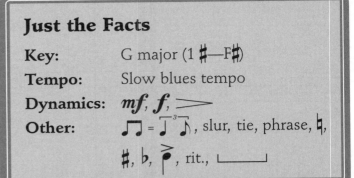

Just the Facts

Key:	G major (1 ♯—F♯)
Tempo:	Slow blues tempo
Dynamics:	*mf*, *f*, >
Other:	♫ = ♩♪, slur, tie, phrase, ♮, ♯, ♭, >, rit., ⌐⌐

W. C. Handy
Arr. by E. L. Lancaster

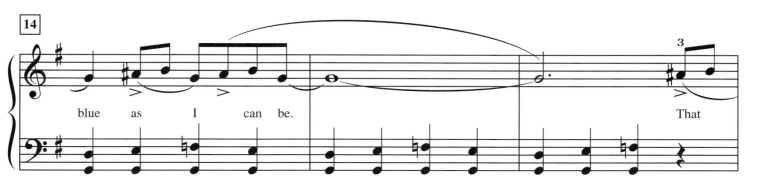

blue   as   I   can   be.   That

man   got   a   heart   like   a   rock   cast   in   the   sea.

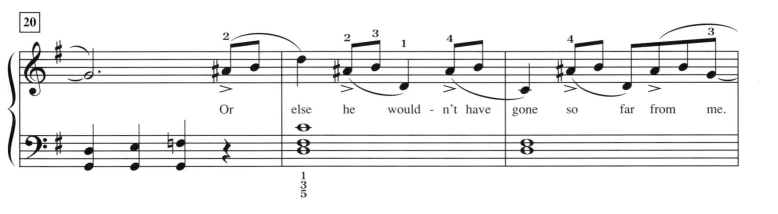

Or   else   he   would - n't   have   gone   so   far   from   me.

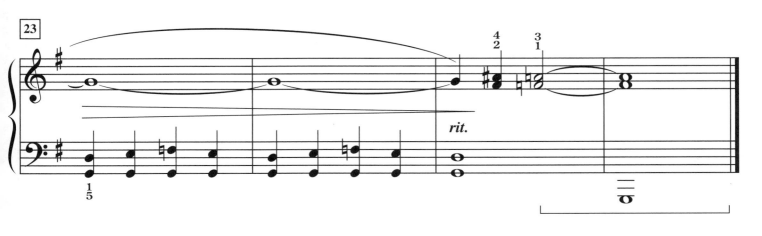

STUDY

For five-finger patterns in LH
and chords in RH

Just the Facts

Key:	C major (no ♯s or ♭s)
Tempo:	Allegro
Dynamics:	*mf*, *f*, <
Other:	Op., slur, tie, ♯, ♮

Jean-Louis Streabbog
Op. 63, No. 2

ÉCOSSAISE

Just the Facts

Key:	G major (1 ♯—F♯)
Tempo:	Allegro
Dynamics:	*p*, *f*
Other:	écossaise, WoO, slur,

écossaise, WoO, slur,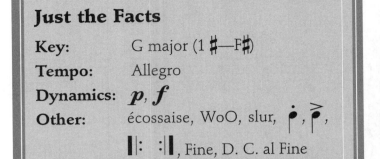

‖: :‖, Fine, D. C. al Fine

Ludwig van Beethoven
WoO 23

VALSE SEMPLICE

<table>
<tr><td colspan="2">Just the Facts</td></tr>
<tr><td>Key:</td><td>G major (1 ♯—F♯)</td></tr>
<tr><td>Tempo:</td><td>Tenderly</td></tr>
<tr><td>Dynamics:</td><td>mp, <, >, mf, f</td></tr>
<tr><td>Other:</td><td>slur, ⌣, phrase, ♭, ♮, rit., a tempo, ♯, //, tie</td></tr>
</table>

Dennis Alexander

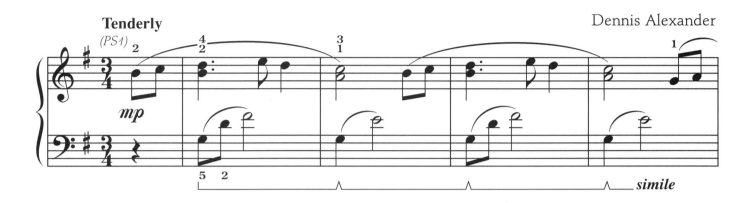

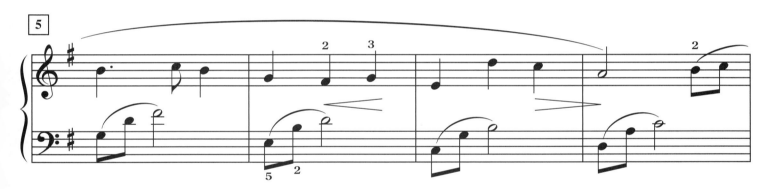

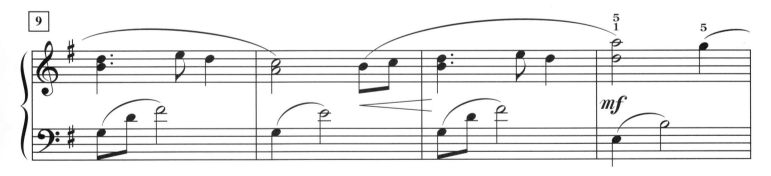

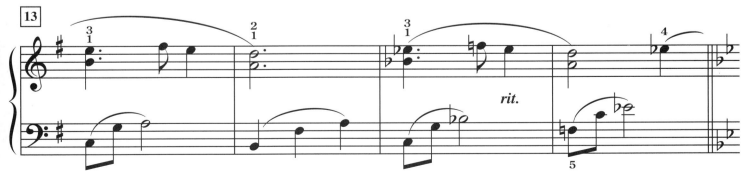

"Valse Semplice" from *Simply Sensational, Book 1,* by Dennis Alexander
Copyright © MCMXCI by Alfred Publishing Co., Inc.

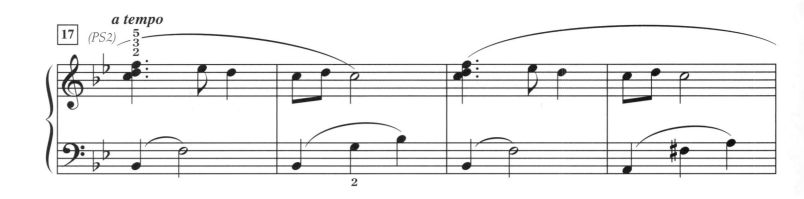

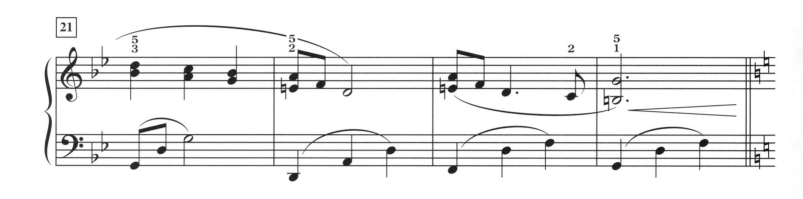

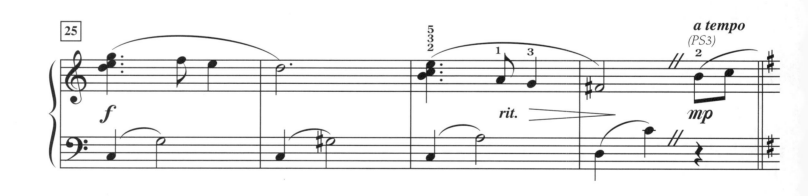

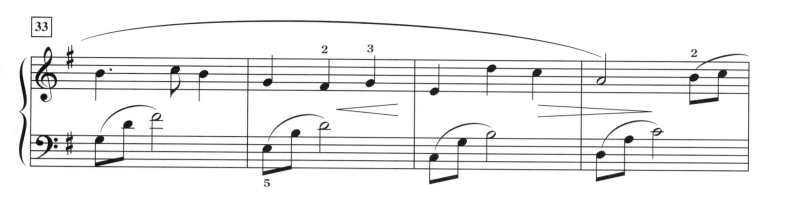

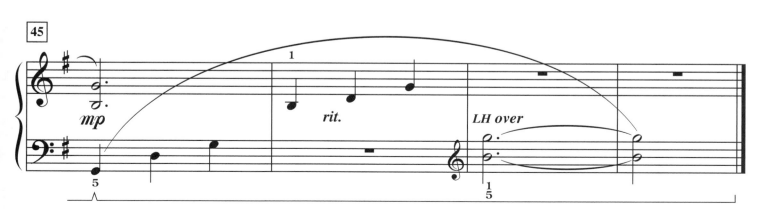

PERSISTENT RHYTHM

Just the Facts

Key:	C minor (3 ♭s—B♭, E♭, A♭)
Tempo:	With a driving beat
Dynamics:	**mp**, <, **mf**, >, **f**, **p**
Other:	phrase, ♯, ♮, tie, , ♭, >, rit.,

With a driving beat (Play ♩♩ evenly)

Martha Mier

"Persistent Rhythm" from *Jazz, Rags & Blues, Book 3*, by Martha Mier
Copyright © MCMXCVI by Alfred Publishing Co., Inc.

Unit Nine

IN THE HALL OF THE MOUNTAIN KING
(from *Peer Gynt Suite*)

Just the Facts

Key:	G minor (2 ♭s—B♭ and E♭)
Tempo:	March tempo
Dynamics:	*pp*, *p*, *mp*, *mf*, cresc., *f*, ⟩
Other:	˙, >̇, ♯, ♮, ♭, 8va

Edvard Grieg
Arr. by E. L. Lancaster

March tempo
(PS1)

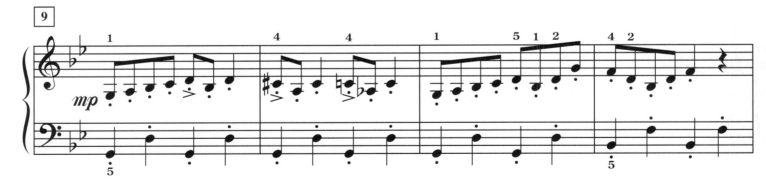

PRELUDE IN C MAJOR

(from *The Well-Tempered Clavier, Book 1*)

Just the Facts

Key:	C major (no ♯s or ♭s)
Tempo:	Andante con moto
Dynamics:	*mp*, *p*, poco cresc., dim., *pp*, cresc. poco a poco, dim. poco a poco
Other:	⌐⌐‿, tie, ♯, ♭, ♮, poco rit., {

Johann Sebastian Bach

Andante con moto

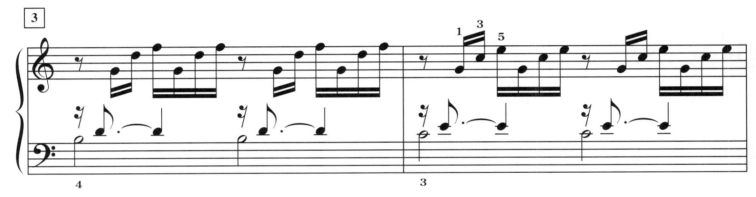

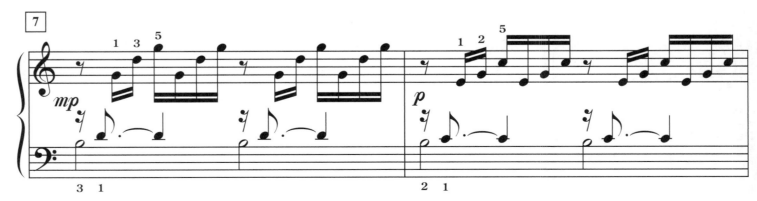

THE ENTERTAINER

<table>
<tr><td colspan="2">Just the Facts</td></tr>
<tr><td>Key:</td><td>C major (no ♯s or ♭s)</td></tr>
<tr><td>Tempo:</td><td>Not fast!</td></tr>
<tr><td>Dynamics:</td><td>f, >, p, <, f, cresc.</td></tr>
<tr><td>Other:</td><td>8va, slur, phrase, tie, 𝅘𝅥, ➤, LH detached, ⌐1.⌐, ⌐2.⌐, :‖</td></tr>
</table>

Scott Joplin
Arr. by E. L. Lancaster

Not fast!

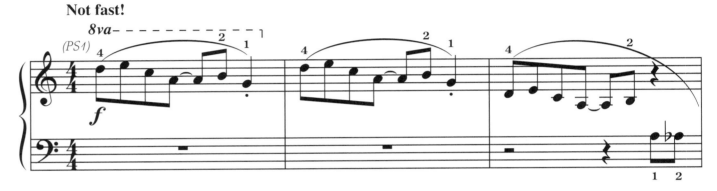

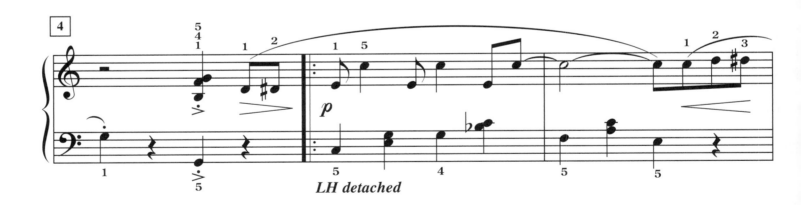

LH detached

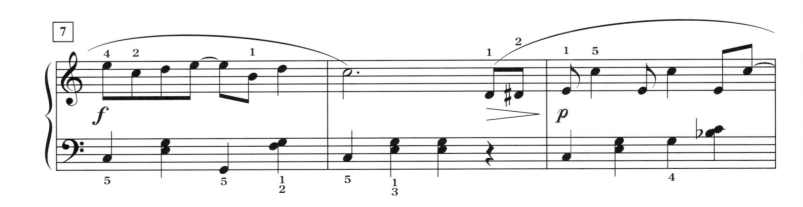

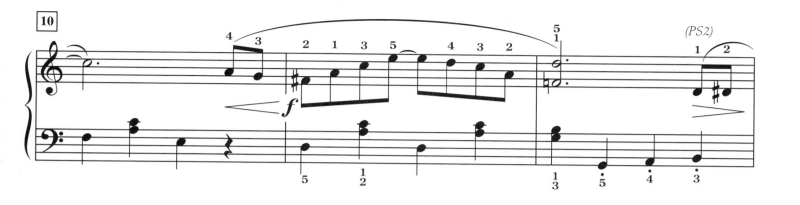

LH detached

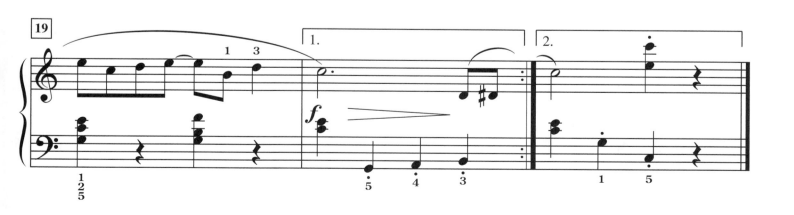

STUDY

For scales in RH and LH

Just the Facts

Key:	C major (no ♯s or ♭s)
Tempo:	Allegretto
Dynamics:	***p***, cresc., ＜, ***f***, ＞
Other:	phrase, ♪̣, slur, ♯, ♮, ***sf***, 8va, ♪̣

Carl Czerny

PRELUDE IN SEVENTHS

Just the Facts

Key: D major (2 ♯s—F♯, C♯)
Tempo: Flowing, with rubato
Dynamics: *mp*, <, >, *f*, *mf*, *p*
Other: ⌐⌐∧, phrase, tie, ♮, ♭, poco rit., to Coda ⊕, a tempo, espressivo e poco più mosso, ♯, D.C. al Coda ⊕, 8va, ⌢

Catherine Rollin

STRUTTIN' COOL

George Peter Tingley

Unit Ten

THEME FROM THE MOONLIGHT SONATA

(First Movement)

Just the Facts

Key: D minor (1 ♭—B♭)
Tempo: Adagio sostenuto
Dynamics: **pp**, <, >, cresc., **p**
Other: sonata, Op., ⌐⌐⌐, slur, ♪♪♪,
            ♭, ♯, ♮, rit.

Ludwig van Beethoven
Op. 27, No. 2
Arr. by E. L. Lancaster

Adagio sostenuto

SONATINA IN C MAJOR
(First Movement)

Muzio Clementi
Op. 36, No. 1

THE HOUSE OF THE RISING SUN

Just the Facts

Key:	E minor (1 ♯—F♯)
Tempo:	Freely, with feeling
Dynamics:	***p***, cresc., >, ***mp***, <, ***mf***, ***f***
Other:	⌐⌐, slur, tie, ♯, simile, ♮, ♭, rit., ⌒, 8va

Traditional
Arr. by E. L. Lancaster

Freely, with feeling

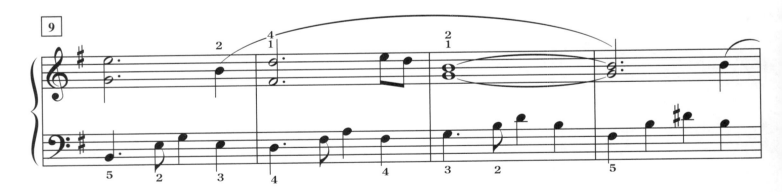

ARABESQUE

For five-finger patterns
and articulation

Just the Facts

Key:	A minor (no ♯s or ♭s)
Tempo:	Allegro scherzando
Dynamics:	*p*, ⟨, *f*
Other:	arabesque, Op., , slur, leggiero, , tie, *sf*,

1. , 2. , ‖: :‖, phrase,
dim. e poco rit., a tempo, dolce, risoluto, ⌢

Johann Friedrich Burgmüller
Op. 100, No. 2

Allegro scherzando

ENCORE ETUDE

Just the Facts

Key:	G minor (2 ♭s—B♭, E♭)
Tempo:	Vivace
Dynamics:	*mp*, *p*, <, *mf*, >, *ff*, *f*
Other:	encore, etude, ⌐⌐, phrase, ♯, ♮, ♭, ⋅, tie, ‾, simile, allargando, ⌢, //, a tempo, 8va, *sff*

Margaret Goldston

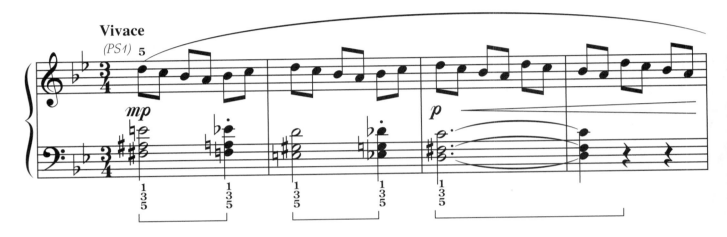

"Encore Etude" from *The Virtuosic Performer, Book 2,* by Margaret Goldston
Copyright © MM by Alfred Publishing Co., Inc.

PINE CONE RAG

Just the Facts

Key:	C major (no ♯s or ♭s)
Tempo:	Steady, moderate tempo
Dynamics:	*f*, *mf*, >, <, *mp*, *ff*
Other:	phrase, ♯, ♭, tie, slur, 2nd time to Coda ⊕, D.S. al Coda ⊕, ⊕ Coda

Steady, moderate tempo (Play ♪♪ evenly)

Martha Mier

(PS1)

2nd time to Coda ⊕

(PS2)

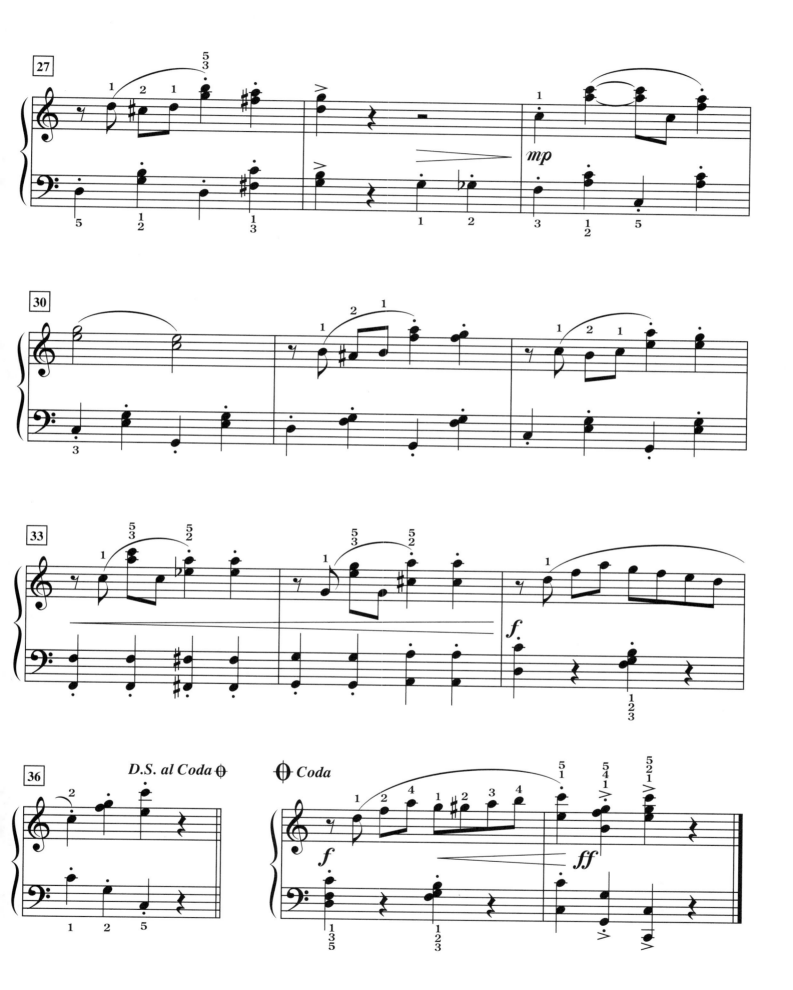

Unit Eleven

CANON

Just the Facts

Key:	C major (no ♯s or ♭s)
Tempo:	Andante
Dynamics:	*p*, <, *mp*, *mf*, *f*, >
Other:	⌐∧⌐, slur, finger substitution **(5–1)**, phrase, ◌̄, poco rit., ⌢

Johann Pachelbel
Arr. by Carol Matz

SPINNING SONG

Just the Facts

Key:	F major (1 ♭—B♭)
Tempo:	Allegretto
Dynamics:	*p*, cresc., *f*, >, <, *mf*
Other:	Op., slur, tie, poco rit., a tempo, phrase, dim. e rit.

Albert Ellmenreich
Op. 14, No. 4

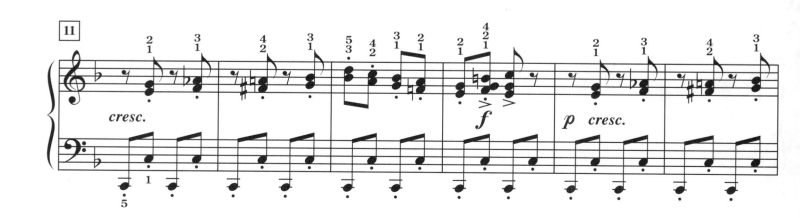

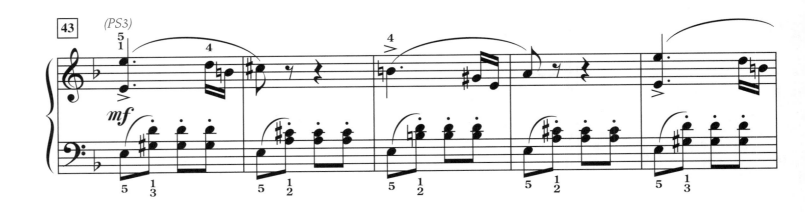

for *Mark J. Sullivan*

DANNY BOY
(*Londonderry Air*)

Irish Folk Song
Arr. by Victoria McArthur

STUDY

For voicing and shaping the
melody in a complex texture

Just the Facts

Key:	G major (1 ♯ — F♯)
Tempo:	Moderato cantabile
Dynamics:	*mf*, cresc., dim., ⟨, ⟩, *mp*, *f*
Other:	Op., ⌣, legato, phrase, ♯, grace note ♪, ♮, slur, tie, ⟩, poco rit., ⌢

Giuseppe Concone
Op. 24, No. 23

ROCK BALLAD

Just the Facts

Key:	A minor (no ♯s or ♭s)
Tempo:	Flowing
Dynamics:	*mp*, *p*, *mf*, cresc., *f*, ⟩
Other:	slur, ⌣∧⌣ , tie, ♯, to Coda ⊕,
	D.S. 𝄋 al Coda, ⊕ Coda, dim. e rit.

Catherine Rollin

* LH to be played detached in measures 9–16.

REVERIE

Just the Facts

Key: D major (2 ♯s—F♯, C♯)

Tempo: Tempo rubato

Dynamics: *p-mp*, cresc., *mf*, >, <, *f*, dim. poco a poco, *pp*, *ppp*

Other: ⌐⌐, slur, tie, simile, ♪♪♪, ♮, phrase, ♭, 𝄾, riten., a tempo, 3rd time to Coda ⊕, rit., grace notes ♫, ♯, rall., D.C. al Coda, ⊕ Coda, una corda, grace note ♪, ⌢

George Peter Tingley

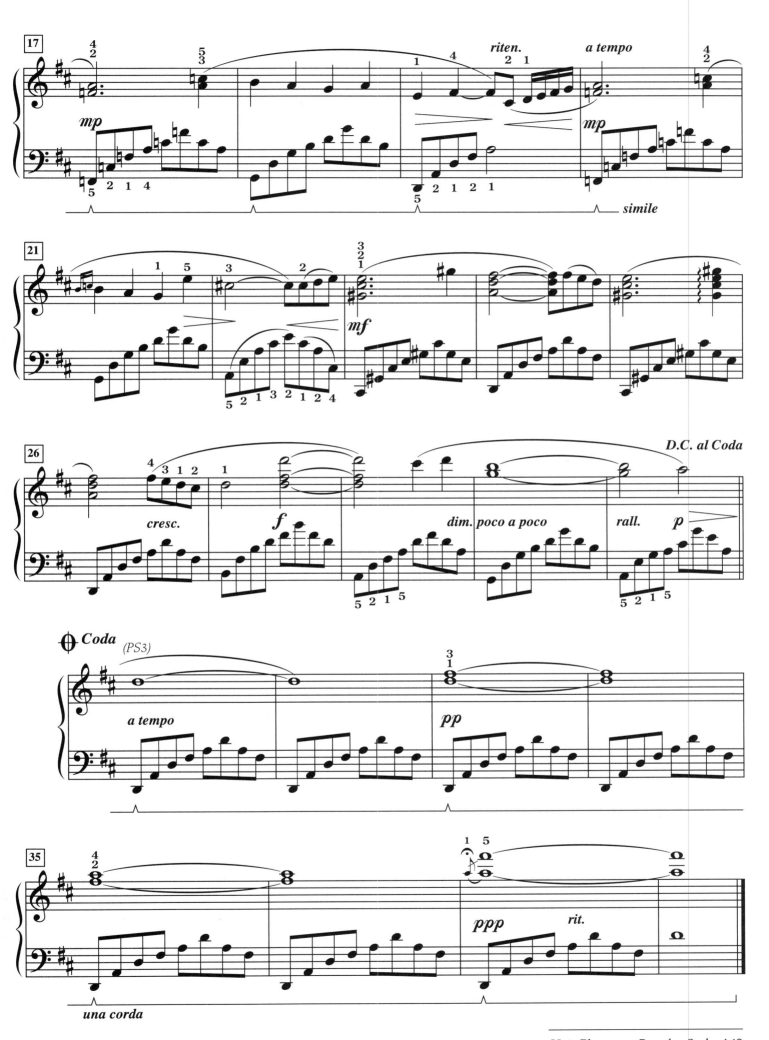

What Do You Remember? Part One—Answer Key

(See pages 10–11.)

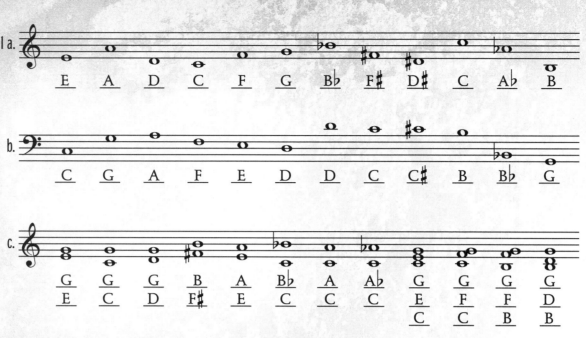

1 a. E A D C F G Bb F# D# C Ab B

b. C G A F E D D C C# B Bb G

c.
G G G B A Bb A Ab G G G G
E C D F# E C C C E F F D
                              C C B B

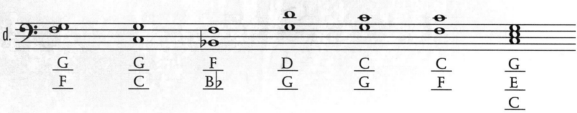

d.
G G F   D C C G
F C Bb G G F E
                   C

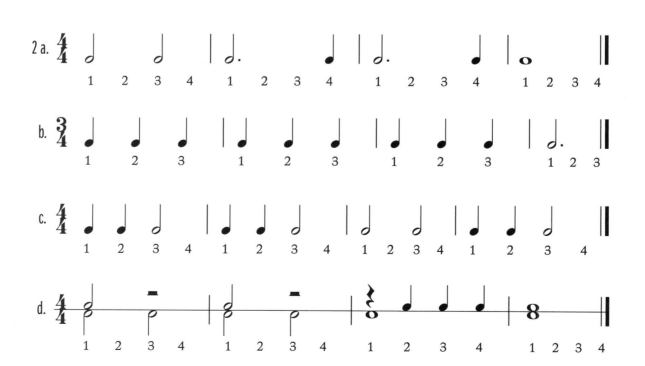

2 a. $\frac{4}{4}$ 𝅗𝅥 𝅗𝅥 𝅗𝅥. ♩ 𝅗𝅥. ♩ 𝅝
       1 2 3 4 1 2 3 4 1 2 3 4 1 2 3 4

b. $\frac{3}{4}$ ♩ ♩ ♩ | ♩ ♩ ♩ | ♩ ♩ ♩ | 𝅗𝅥.
       1 2 3 1 2 3 1 2 3 1 2 3

c. $\frac{4}{4}$ ♩ ♩ ♩ | ♩ ♩ ♩ | 𝅗𝅥 𝅗𝅥 | ♩ ♩ 𝅗𝅥
       1 2 3 4 1 2 3 4 1 2 3 4 1 2 3 4

d. $\frac{4}{4}$ 𝅗𝅥 ― | 𝅗𝅥 ― | 𝄽 ♩ ♩ ♩ | 𝅝
       1 2 3 4 1 2 3 4 1 2 3 4 1 2 3 4

What Do You Remember? Part Two—Answer Key

(See pages 12–13.)

What Do You Remember? Part Three—Answer Key

(See pages 14–15.)

What Do You Remember? Part Four——Answer Key

(See pages 16–17.)

About the Composers and Arrangers

Dennis Alexander (b. 1947) is an independent piano teacher in Northridge, California. A graduate of the University of Kansas, he was on the faculty of the University of Montana for 24 years where he taught applied piano, group piano and piano pedagogy.

Johann Sebastian Bach (1685–1750) is the most famous composer from the Baroque period and perhaps of all time. He came from a family of musicians who were active as composers, performers and teachers. Bach was a famous organist during his time, and much of his music was written for the church as well as for teaching purposes.

Ludwig van Beethoven (1770–1827), the famous German composer, is known throughout the world for his creative genius. His symphonies, concertos, chamber music and piano sonatas are recognized as his greatest masterpieces. Beginning in 1802, he experienced hearing loss and was completely deaf before the end of his life; however, he continued his energetic compositional process without interruption.

Ferdinand Beyer (1803–1863), a German, was best known for his arrangements of music originally written for orchestra and opera. He wrote a comprehensive piano method that is still used by teachers today.

Alexander Borodin (1833–1887) was a Russian composer who earned a doctorate in chemistry. Although trained as a scientist, he composed throughout his lifetime. Several of his works, including the opera *Prince Igor,* were incomplete at his death and were completed by Russian colleagues.

Johann Friedrich Burgmüller (1806–1874) was a German piano teacher and composer of salon pieces and piano studies for children. He settled in Paris in 1832 and became a French citizen. His piano studies have achieved pedagogical prominence due to their melodic appeal and technical considerations.

Jeremiah Clarke (c.1673–1707) was an English composer and organist. He composed church music, songs, incidental music for the theater and harpsichord pieces. He held organ positions at Winchester College and at St. Paul's Cathedral in London.

Muzio Clementi (1752–1832) was an Italian teacher, pianist and composer. He was educated in England where he lived most of his life. In addition, he established a successful publishing company and piano factory. He toured as a concert pianist, taught many outstanding musicians and wrote numerous symphonies, piano sonatas and etudes.

Giuseppe Concone (1801–1861), an Italian, was mainly known as a teacher of singing as well as a composer of vocal studies and other pieces for singers, including two operas. He also was an organist and choir master as well as a composer of piano studies.

Carl Czerny (1791–1857) was an Austrian pianist, teacher and composer. He taught only talented students and devoted the remainder of his time to composition and arranging. He published almost 1,000 compositions during his lifetime, with numerous manuscripts left unpublished.

Claude Debussy (1862–1918), a French composer, is considered the creator of musical Impressionism. At the age of 10, he entered the Paris Conservatory where he studied piano, solfege and harmony. He greatly influenced 20th-century music through his use of modes, whole-tone and pentatonic scales, tonal ambiguity, unresolved chords and parallel intervals.

Albert Ellmenreich (1816–1905) is the composer of the popular teaching piece "Spinning Song." Very little is known about him. It is possible that he was a German actor and composer of opera in the court theater at Schwerin.

Margaret Goldston (b. 1932) is an independent piano teacher in Franklin, North Carolina. A graduate of Louisiana State University, she is widely known as a composer and arranger of educational music for piano students.

Edvard Grieg (1843–1907) is remembered as a nationalistic composer from Norway. In his music, he was able to capture the melodic and rhythmic flavor of Norwegian folk songs. His best compositions are miniatures, including several lyric pieces for piano, and songs that were frequently performed by his wife Nina Hagerup, a well-known singer.

Cornelius Gurlitt (1820–1901), was a German organist, teacher, and student of the composer Carl Reinecke (1824–1910). Best known as a composer, Gurlitt authored over 250 works, many of which continue to be played by students today.

W. C. Handy (1873–1958), an African-American composer and cornet player, is often called the "Father of the Blues." Born in Florence, Alabama, he was a schoolteacher and worked in the iron mills before touring the South and conducting his own orchestra. He is credited with turning ragtime into a more ballad-like style by lowering the third, fifth and seventh scale tones to create "blue notes."

Charles-Louis Hanon (1819–1900) was a French organist and choir director at the Eglise Saint-Joseph in Bologne-sur-Mer. After leaving his church position, he remained in Bologne and taught piano and voice. His fame as a composer rests solely on the popularity of his exercises for pianists called *The Virtuoso Pianist.*

Randall Hartsell (b. 1949) lives in Charlotte, North Carolina, where he is active as a teacher, composer, accompanist, clinician, adjudicator and church organist/conductor. A native of North Carolina, he is a graduate of East Carolina University.

Franz Joseph Haydn (1732–1809), an Austrian, is one of the most famous composers from the Classical period. He is widely recognized for his contributions to the development and evolution of the symphony. His compositional output is enormous and his total contributions will never be known since many works are lost or of doubtful authenticity.

Scott Joplin (1868–1917) was an African-American pianist and composer. His fame is based on his 50 piano rags, the first success being the "Maple Leaf Rag," composed in 1899. In addition, he wrote two operas. Joplin's popularity increased in 1974 with the release of the movie *The Sting,* which featured his music.

Louis Köhler (1820–1886) was a German conductor, teacher and critic, as well as a composer of over 300 works, most of which were piano etudes written for his own students. In 1847 he started a music school that became very successful.

Gayle Kowalchyk (b. 1955) is Keyboard Editor for Supplementary Piano Publications for Alfred Publishing Company. A former faculty member at Eastern Illinois University, she is the co-author of more than 100 educational piano books.

E. L. Lancaster (b. 1948) is Vice President and Keyboard Editor-in-Chief of Alfred Publishing Company. In 1980, he established the masters and doctoral programs in piano pedagogy at the University of Oklahoma, where he was a faculty member from 1979–1998.

Adolphe-Clair Le Carpentier (1809–1869), a French pianist and composer, graduated from the Paris Conservatory. He published a piano method for children, collections of etudes, and fantasies based on operatic themes.

Carol Matz (b. 1965) is an independent piano teacher in Hollywood, Florida and a keyboard editor for Alfred Publishing Company. She attended the University of Miami and studied composition, arranging and orchestration with an emphasis on studio and jazz writing.

Victoria McArthur (b. 1949) is Program Director of Piano Pedagogy and Coordinator of Group Piano at Florida State University, Tallahassee. She is a keyboard editor for Alfred Publishing Company and has authored or co-authored over 40 educational piano publications.

Martha Mier (b. 1936) is an independent piano teacher in Lake City, Florida. A graduate of Florida State University, she is an active clinician and adjudicator. Her educational piano music for students of all levels has made her one of today's most popular composers.

Jean-Joseph Mouret (1682–1738) was a French composer who was employed by the court in Paris. He also directed the orchestra at the Paris Opera. His *Suites de Symphonies* were originally scored for a small ensemble.

Wolfgang Amadeus Mozart (1756–1791), an Austrian, is known throughout the world as one of the greatest musical geniuses of all time. As a young child, he concertized extensively, sometimes playing duets with his sister Nannerl. He wrote music for all genres, including opera and other stage works, symphonies and other orchestral music, concertos, chamber music, and solo keyboard works

Johann Pachelbel (1653–1706) was a German composer, organist and teacher. He was a friend of the Bach family and the teacher of Johann Christoph Bach (1671–1721). He is known for his organ chorales, non-liturgical keyboard music and vocal music.

Sergei Rachmaninoff (1873–1943) was widely known as a composer and pianist. Born in Russia, he became an American citizen a few weeks before his death in Beverly Hills, California. His music is rooted in the Romantic tradition of the 19th century and his piano works have broad melodic lines and rich harmonies.

Jean-Philippe Rameau (1683–1764) was a French composer, theorist and organist. He is credited with creating harmonic structures that are still used today, including triads and inversions. His operas dominated the French stage for many years.

Catherine Rollin (b. 1952) is an independent teacher in Bloomfield Hills, Michigan. A teacher of prize-winning students, she received her Bachelor of Musical Arts degree from the University of Michigan and her Master of Music degree from Oakland University.

Ludvig Schytte (1848–1909), a Danish composer, was a pharmacist before he began his music training at the age of 22. His teachers included the respected composers Niels Gade (1817–1890) and Franz Liszt (1811–1886). He taught at music conservatories in Berlin and Vienna where he composed mainly for piano.

Jean-Louis Streabbog (1835–1886), a Belgian composer, was actually Jean-Louis Gobbaerts. "Streabbog" is "Gobbaerts" spelled backwards. Gobbaerts wrote under several other pen names, including Lecocq, Ludovic and Levy. He is best known for his piano salon pieces.

Albert Von Tilzer (1873–1956) was an American songwriter and publisher. "Von" was added to his mother's maiden name, Tilzer, to form his professional pseudonym. His music is representative of early 20th century Tin Pan Alley, and many of his songs are considered traditional favorites.

George Peter Tingley (b. 1950) is a composer, teacher and pianist from Point Richmond, California, in the San Francisco Bay Area. He is a graduate of California State University, Hayward, and the University of Southern California. In the 1970s, he was a private composition student of the legendary Nadia Boulanger in Paris, France.

Heinrich Wohlfahrt (1797–1883) was a piano teacher, writer and composer who lived in Leipzig, Germany. He is best known for his piano music for students.

Glossary

Tempo (speed of the piece of music)

Adagio sostenuto	a slow tempo, slower than *andante* and faster than *lento*
Allegretto	moderately fast; a little slower than *allegro*
Allegro	fast; lively
Allegro moderato	moderately fast
Allegro scherzando	fast in a joking, playful style
Andante	moving along; walking speed
Andante cantabile	moving along in a singing style
Andante con moto	moving along with motion
Andantino	slightly faster than *andante*
Moderato	moderately
Tempo rubato	with slight changes in the tempo for expressive purposes
Vivace	lively, quick

Dynamics (degrees of loudness or softness)

cresc. or <	Crescendo	gradually louder
decresc. or >	Decrescendo	gradually softer (same as *dim.*)
dim. or >	Diminuendo	gradually softer (same as *decresc.*)
f	Forte	loud
ff	Fortissimo	very loud
mf	Mezzo forte	moderately loud
mp	Mezzo piano	moderately soft
pp	Pianissimo	very soft
ppp	Pianississimo	very, very soft
p	Piano	soft
p—mp	Piano—mezzo piano	soft the first time and moderately soft on the repeat

Other

𝆓	Accent sign	placed over or under a note to be played louder
	Allargando	becoming slower
♪	Appoggiatura	an ornament, usually played on the beat
	Arabesque	a piece in a florid, decorative style
	Arpeggio	notes of a chord are sounded successively rather than together
	A tempo	resume previous speed
	Cadence	a group of chords that establishes the tonal center of a piece
//	Caesura	indicates a sudden pause
	Cantabile	in a singing style

	Cantata	a multi-movement work for chorus and/or soloist(s) with orchestra
	Chord	three or more notes sounded together
𝄌	Coda	ending section of a movement or piece
	Con	with
	Concerto	a piece for orchestra and solo instrument
	Con moto	with motion; faster
D.C. al Coda	Da Capo al Coda	repeat from the beginning to the 𝄌
D.C. al Fine	Da Capo al Fine	repeat from the beginning to the word *Fine*
D.S. al Coda	Dal Segno al Coda	repeat from the sign 𝄋 to the 𝄌
⎩⎭ or ⎩⋀⎭	Damper pedal	depress the right pedal
	Dolce	sweetly
	Dorian	a mode (scale) that corresponds to the pattern of whole and half steps created when playing from D to D on the white keys of the piano
e		and
	Écossaise	a country dance usually in $\frac{2}{4}$ time
	Encore	a short, often fast piece played at the end of a performance in response to audience applause
	Espressivo	expressive
	Etude	a study or technical exercise
𝄐	Fermata	hold the note longer than its full value
Fine	Fine	the end
5–1, *etc.*	Finger substitution	play the note with the first finger indicated, then silently change to the next finger indicated
1.	First ending	play first time only
	Five-finger pattern	first five notes of a scale
♭	Flat	lowers the note one half step; play the next key to the left, whether black or white
♪ ♫	Grace note(s)	small ornamental note(s), generally played quickly before the beat

	Key	the tonal center of a piece, defined by the scale from which the pitches are drawn
	Legato	smoothly connected
	Leggiero	lightly
	LH detached	left-hand notes are separated
	Major	a mode (scale) that corresponds to the patterns of whole and half steps created when playing from C to C on the white keys of the piano; can also refer to chords and intervals
	Minor	a mode (scale) that corresponds to the patterns of whole and half steps created when playing from A to A on the white keys of the piano (natural minor); can also refer to chords and intervals
	Minuet	an elegant dance in $\frac{3}{4}$ time
	Mosso	movement
	Moto	motion
	Musette	a piece of dance music with a repeated, drone accompaniment
♮	**Natural**	cancels a sharp or flat
8va	**Octave**	play eight scale tones (one octave) higher when the sign is above the note(s); play eight scale tones lower when the sign is below the note(s)
Op.	**Opus**	work; chronological number given to a composition
	Phrase	a musical thought; often indicated by a slur
	Più	more
	Poco	little
	Poco a poco	little by little
	Poco rit. or **poco rall.**	slowing a little
	Prelude	a short work for piano
	Quadrille	a 19th-century dance for four or more couples
rall.	**Rallentando**	gradually slowing (same as *rit.*)
‖: :‖	**Repeat sign**	repeat from the beginning or from the first repeat sign ‖:
	Risoluto	bold; with determination

rit.	**Ritardando**	gradually slowing (same as *rall.*)
riten.	**Ritenuto**	immediately slower; held back
	Rolled chord	rolled or arpeggiated chord, bottom to top
	Rondeau	the French term for a piece of music with alternation of a main section with other sections
	Rondino	a small rondo (see *rondeau*)
	Rubato	slight changes in tempo for expressive purposes
	Scale	a group of notes arranged in order from lowest to highest or vice versa; most common scales are major and minor
2.	**Second ending**	play second time only
sf or *sff*	**Sforzando**	a sudden, strong accent
♯	**Sharp**	raises the note one half step; play the next key to the right, whether black or white
sim.	**Simile**	continue in the same manner
	Slur	curved line over or under notes on different lines or spaces, meaning to play legato
	Sonata	a composition for one or more instruments, usually multi-movement, prevalent beginning in the 17th century
	Sonatina	a short, sometimes simple, sonata
	Staccato	detached; indicated by a dot over or under the note
	Tenuto	hold the note for its full value; sometimes a slight emphasis
	Tie	a curved line joining notes on the same line or space; hold for the combined value of both notes
	To next strain	skip to next section
	Transpose	to perform in a key other than the original
	Triplet	three notes played in the time of two notes of the same kind
u.c.	**Una corda**	soft pedal (on the left); "one string"
WoO	**Without opus**	work without opus number
	With swing	play eighth notes a bit unevenly, in a "lilting" style; long-short, long-short, etc.

List of Compositions (Alphabetical by Title)